Good Hello Calm

Insights to Soothe the Soul

Laura Loveberry
Author   Speaker   Life Coach

Silent Witness, LLM Publications
Printed in the U.S.A.

Laura Loveberry

GOODBYE CHAOS HELLO CALM

Copyright Notice   *Goodbye Chaos Hello Calm*, Inspirational Nonfiction   First edition. Copyright © 2024 by Laura Loveberry. The information contained in this book is the intellectual property of Laura Loveberry and is governed by U. S. and the International Copyright laws. All rights reserved. No part of this publications, either text or image, may be used for any purpose other than personal use.

The *Goodbye Chaos Hello Calm* book gleans from a collection of *Life is the Berries* articles from *Simply Hers*, *Everything Men*, and *Simply Senior* magazines published by *Chestney Publishing*. (www.simplyhersmagazine.net) Marlanea McGraw of Chestney Publishing and author Laura loveberry, have an agreement for Laura Loveberry to modify, compile, arrange, and publish as a book *"Life is the Berries"* articles to create the *Goodbye Chaos Hello Calm* book.

Cover and Design: Laura Loveberry and Patrick Cook.   Layout: Lisa Cook
Editors: Rosalie Currier

"Scripture quotations taken from the New American Standard Bible® (NASB), Copyright © 1960, 1962, 1963, 1968, 1971, 1972, 1973, 1975, 1977, 1995 by The Lockman Foundation Used by permission. www.Lockman.org"

"Scripture quotations taken from the Amplified® Bible (AMP), Copyright © 2015 by The Lockman Foundation. Used by permission. www.Lockman.org"

The Living Bible copyright © 1971 by Tyndale House Foundation. Used by permission of Tyndale House Publishers Inc., Carol Stream, Illinois 60188. All rights reserved. The Living Bible, TLB, and The Living Bible logo are registered trademarks of Tyndale House Publishers.

Scripture quotations marked MSG are taken from *THE MESSAGE*, copyright © 1993, 2002, 2018 by Eugene H. Peterson. Used by permission of NavPress. All rights reserved. Represented by Tyndale House Publishers, Inc.

THE HOLY BIBLE, NEW INTERNATIONAL VERSION®, NIV® Copyright © 1973, 1978, 1984, 2011 by Biblica, Inc.® Used by permission. All rights reserved worldwide.

Scripture marked NKJV taken from the New King James Version®. Copyright © 1982 by Thomas Nelson. Used by permission. All rights reserved.

Scripture quotations marked NLT are taken from the *Holy Bible*, New Living Translation, copyright © 1996, 2004, 2015 by Tyndale House Foundation. Used by permission of Tyndale House Publishers, Inc., Carol Stream, Illinois 60188. All rights reserved.

Publisher: *Silent Witness, LLM.*
ISBN # 979-8-9886500-6-5

www.lauraloveberry.com

PRINTED IN THE U.S.A.

"I love it! Readers will connect with Laura's tenacious faith, earthiness, and humor. Her great content will grab readers."

Ann Spangler, *Award-winning Writer & Best-selling Author*

"Such a happy book - humorous and heartfelt. Laura's a master at helping to overcome with practical encouragement to live life fully—no matter what the circumstances. We all get mud-splattered by life and need a shower of inspiration and humor to press on."

Robyn Dykstra, *National Christian Speaker & Best-Selling Author*

"Laura's wit and wisdom help us through our hard season! Buy a bunch of books and give them to encourage friends and family."

Regina Mae, *Singer, Songwriter, Nashville Recording Artist*

Laura Loveberry

DEDICATION
Mark Loveberry

I dedicate this book to my hubster, Mark. One dark night, we crested over a hill. Slamming on the brakes without warning, he spins a 180° turn, whipping to an abrupt halt. Appearing like a ghost, a white stallion stands alone in the middle of the road. Jumping out of the car, Mark coaxes the massive horse closer. He grabs the bridle, walking the escaped steed back to the owner's farmhouse.

I sit wide-eyed, shaking.

I married this modern-day-knight-in-shining-armor.

When not rescuing me from near collisions, he listens to my rough drafts, laughs at my humorous articles, and insists I never divulge our craziest stories. Mark encourages me mightily to write to inspire readers.

He remains the calm in my chaos.

Laura Loveberry

APPRECIATION

Ann Spangler

Marlanea McGraw

I appreciate the professional insight from Ann Spangler, the best-selling author. She gifted her valuable time to advise me. Sitting down over brunch, this accomplished writer shared her prolific knowledge on the craft of writing. I scribbled voracious notes between bites. Later, checking out my book draft, Ann emailed worthy suggestions, pegged a better title, and offered to allow me to quote her positive comments on my writing. It's a remarkable boost to any author when Ann Spangler declares, "I love it!"

I want to thank Marlanea McGraw, my dear friend and owner/publisher/CEO of *Simply Hers*, *Everything Men,* and *Simply Senior* magazines. Years ago, Marlanea requested I write spiritual articles in her secular magazine. I plunged deep into the opportunity, calling myself the CSO, Chief Spiritual Officer. She jumpstarted the writer within me. This book gleans from my years of encouraging our magazine readers.

Laura Loveberry

INTRODUCTION

"Now the Lord of peace Himself give you peace always by all means. The Lord be with you all."
2 Thes. 3:16 KJV

Hello to tranquility and peace.

For my friends striving in the hustle and bustle, I invite us to share selah moments in standalone chapters. Let's laugh, love, and learn together.

Let's open the door to our reset, our renewal, our recharge. We can revive! I invite you inside. Welcome. I'm happy you're here. Enjoy!

Thanks for joining me,

Laura Loveberry

Laura Loveberry

Laugh It Off

*". . . fill thy mouth with laughing
and thy lips with rejoicing."*
Job 8:21b KJV

The unexpected smacks you when you least suspect.

One lovely morning, I was diapering my newborn on our couch. Fellow moms told me girls are easier to change as they do not shoot streams of pee pee like baby boys.

First, I remove my daughter's wet diaper. Lifting both legs gently with one hand, I slide the clean diaper under her itty-bitty buns. Immersing in the tender moment, I soak in the preciousness of a momma with her newborn.

Baby girls exude sweetness.

She and I resemble the models in a Mary Cassatt mother and daughter painting. Bending closer, cooing, I whisper lullabies.

KERSPLAT!

Shooting out of my precious infant's derriere, without warning, bursts globs of stank diarrhea. Not just a little. No. We are talking projectile poop.

It hits my hair. It's rancid. It splats my face. It reeks. It even splatters my mouth. It's rotten. My face got "fecalled." Is that a word? I do not know, but I am fecal face. And it's foul-smelling. It drips off my lips!

Poop splats.

Unexpected things slap us in the face.

Isn't it best to laugh when the doodoo hits the fan . . . or the lips? The Bible says, *"He will once again fill your mouth with laughter and your lips with shouts of joy,"* (Job 8:21 NLT).

Laughter is good, like shouts of joy. We can clean up our messes either giggling or crying. I choose to find the humor as quickly as possible when chaos hits me out of nowhere.

When splatted unexpectedly, just repeat to yourself, "Poop dee doo happens." Recognize the comicalness of the mess and laugh out loud.

Life drops stink bombs.

Learning to laugh helps us get through. What are you going to do? Let's laugh. Let's find the funny. Let's see the silly in the situation.

Here's the scoop when you're covered in poop—you just got to LAUGH.

Our reaction to the startling moment matters. We can choose to solve or sulk, to fix or fuss, to laugh or cry. We can grab responsibility or pass blame.

We can regret the past and stay stuck, or grow grit and climb from the pit. We will repeat mistakes, or we will learn, for goodness sakes.

Poop splatters.

Life spatters. And it matters how we deal with stinky situations. The majority of our life is made from our reaction to the mayhem. Our responses comprise the bulk of our being.

Finding the calm in the chaos inspired the following chapters. I wrote with our muddled messes in mind. Flipping through, you will find discussion questions in the back of the book. For personal introspection and application, readers can answer these life questions individually. Some may want to gather book-reading friends together for deep discussions.

Questions are open-ended, designed for personal reflection, growth, and calming our chaos.

I pray this provides a page-turning encouragement for you, like I aspired in my first book, *Invite Delight, Insights to Sweeten the Soul.* I hope you enjoy this second volume in the series like a dew-drenched strawberry fresh off the vine. My third book in the set is a novel, titled *Bowl of Berries Book Club.* You may delight in its sisterhood, linking these three books together.

I hope you savor this soothing read, chapter by chapter, to the satisfying end.

Turning the last page, I pray you breathe in tranquility, exhaling calamity, saying out loud, "GOODBYE CHAOS. HELLO CALM."

Goodbye Chaos Hello Calm

Laura Loveberry

Hot Potato

"Always be humble and gentle. Be patient with each other, making allowance for each other's faults because of your love."
Eph. 4:2 NLT

Our dinner potatoes bake while Mark and I smooch on our honeymoon at the family cabin. We sidetrack. *Wink. Wink.* I forget my hubster isn't the only smoldering thing in the Loveberry Lodge.

Then we notice smoke billowing out of the oven.

We jolt up from our snuggles.

Dashing for the smoking stove, yanking open the oven door, we toss the flaming potatoes outside. Dousing water on the fire, we dissolve into laughter at our actual "hot potato" game. Mark consoles me for charring our first feast together as husband and wife.

He did not marry me for my cooking.

What a fiery fiasco!

Waking up the next morning, my hubster struts shirtless around the cabin in his pajama bottoms. Sliding open the back door all manly, he steps out, striking a Tarzan-king-of-the-jungle pose. Mark swaggers a morning stretch around the back deck barefooted until . . .

YOUCH!

Suddenly, he hops on one foot, grasping his other foot. Blood gushes out of his heel. Stripped of his manly mood, he shouts for a towel.

Scrambling, I find and throw a dishcloth to him. He stumbles in the door, foot wrapped in the blood-stained towel. What on earth cut so deeply?

The deck looks like a crime scene.

Gently, Mark pulls a black potato skin out of his bloodied foot. We slowly turn. Our eyes meet.

We both smirk.

My potatoes!

The sizzled-sharp potato skins, from the night before, had hardened, slicing his foot open, causing this cuisine catastrophe!

We bust out laughing.

All this to say, now we work better together.

When cooking, I often get sidetracked. It ends up in dinner disasters. Our children think the smoke detector is their dinner bell.

Nowadays, we team up in the kitchen.

"Two are better than one, because they have a good return for their labor: If either of them falls down, one can help the other up . . ." (Ecclesiastes 4:9-10a NIV).

We make meals better together now.

We don't mock and snark at mistakes. Mark and I find the humor in the hardly edible. We forgive the food failures. We laugh over lost lunches.

Our kitchen is for dining, dancing, romancing . . . and laughter.

Mark mutilated his foot on our honeymoon, but he did not scar my heart. A critical spirit would have crushed me, instead we work side by side encouraging each other. Our teamwork makes the dreamwork in the kitchen and beyond.

However, I don't recommend going barefoot.

365-Day Gift

". . . we have not stopped praying for you.
We continually ask God to fill you with
the knowledge of his will . . . "
Col. 1:9b NIV

Do you have a prodigal adult child refusing to have contact with you? Has it been going on for years? Are you banned from visiting? Do you long for connection and relationship with a family member who wants nothing to do with you?

We cannot always control these heart-wrenching situations. We cry out to God for healing in these relationships. You and I can seek wisdom and discernment on how best to handle the desperate circumstances. We can speak words of truth to renew our minds with Bible verses such as, "Though He slay me, yet will I trust him . . ." (Job 13:15a KJV).

My friend's estranged son separated from his mom. It slashed her heart daily. She longed for restoration.

I sent the distraught momma the following message. (I changed her name for privacy.)

> *"Dear Sue,*
>
> *I heard this idea I would like to do for my kids to give them a legacy of love, but I think it will be perfect for you and your son who separated himself from the family.*
>
> *Get a Bible with room on the sides for notes. Take this year, reading through the Bible every day, writing out prayers to your son in the margin. Write his specific name throughout.*
>
> *This will be the sweetest gift for him to know you love and keep him in prayers, journaling through a Bible specifically for him. It will give you a positive way to stay connected in the "waiting room of separation."*
>
> *When the time is right, you can bless him with a 365-day gift Bible, personalized*

*with prayers and dreams for him from
your heart.*

*God can do immeasurably more than we
ask or imagine. You may like this idea. I
love it for my kids and grandkids. Love
you. You keep climbing!*

-Laura"

She responded with "hugs" and gratitude.

Prayerfully, she will warrior onward with a mission to
love unconditionally in a practical way, even in the
valley of hard separation.

I cannot think of a more precious gift than the WORD
of GOD and 365 days
of hand-written love
and prayers.

*"So we have not
stopped praying for you
. . ."* (Col. 1:9a NLT).

This gift idea can be for
anyone anytime.

Currently, I am writing
notes in a Bible for my
special-needs daughter.
I hope it will be a
pathway of spiritual

A Bible with
prayers &
mentor notes
in the margin
for the
recipient is
an heirloom.

encouragement. My prayer is she will draw strength from God's Word and know I wrap her in my prayers.

Who do you want to leave a legacy of your love and God's Word?

Perhaps today, you will pick up a Bible with wide margins and join the journey of journaling prayers through a Bible to give to YOUR special someone.

It's like giving a big biblical bearhug every morning!

Surprise Visitor

"He creates each of us by Christ Jesus to join him in the work he does, the good work he has gotten ready for us to do, work we had better be doing."
Eph. 2:10 MSG

A man walks right up to where you sit reading this book, starting a conversation with you.

"Hey, I commission you with an assignment. Can you put down your book for a moment so we can talk face to face without distractions? My mission for you is mighty, not for the weak-hearted," he states.

Startled, you glance up, lowering your book.

He continues the conversation with penetrating eye contact, saying, *"I desire for you to accept my high-calling charge I give you."*

Your eyes open wider and wider.

Staring in disbelief with a dropped jaw, your mind races in total bewilderment, stunned completely.

Jesus stands in front of you.

He wears a robe from biblical days and scars on his pierced hands. Does he grab your modern-day attention? Oh, yeah! His eyes pierce into your soul when he speaks. His hand rests gently on your shoulder.

Engulfed in his presence, you listen as he says,

> *My mission is not an easy road. It is a demanding, rigorous route, riddled with exhaustion. You may think you cannot carry on. But I will remain right with you the entire way—in your pain, doubts, and exhaustion on this quest.*
>
> *You can talk to me along the journey.*
>
> *I call on you to share with seekers my life-changing power. I can set people free and restore relationships. My followers can live in spiritual peace, no matter how horrific their situation may be. I desire for you to share the spiritual source to set their lives ablaze in the dismal times.*
>
> *I will give you unexplainable peace, passing all understanding. You will be a*

carrier of hope to the hopeless, of life to the dying, and of light to a dark world.

So many search for "MORE" in life, coming up feeling empty with less fulfillment.

I am the "MORE" they seek. It's not the things, tone-fit bodies, youth restoring potions, fancy cars, big houses, or the next high-tech gadget.

I am the "MORE."

I am the full answer to their emptiness. I call on you to speak my truths to a confused, misdirected, lost people.

Find them.

Tell them I love them where they are.

Speak to them in the box stores, at the ball games, in the grocery store, at the party. I love people and long for them to come to me broken, ready for a restored purpose in this life I created for each one.

People are my masterpiece creation.

I created them to do the purposeful works I planned for them long ago. People miss out on their God-purpose life.

I charge you to tell them I love them, longing for a genuine relationship with everyone. I desire for humans to experience the "MORE" they are missing.

By the way, people will laugh at you.

They will mock you, tell lies about you, ban you, and attempt to stop my mission. You keep loving and praying for even the ones who reject you and me. They get confused by clever lies against my honest purpose.

Your commission from me, the Son of God, with scarred hands, urges you to LOVE GOD and LOVE PEOPLE.

Go tell everyone you see about me.

I love them. I love you.

> **Jesus is the "MORE" people are looking for.**

Will you take on My charge?

This fictional illustration carries a lot to process, right? In modern living, do we all

Goodbye Chaos Hello Calm

receive this historic-type charge?

Perhaps we don't literally see the ancient robe, scarred hands, or the Jesus in the flesh, but we can be like Jesus with human skin to others. *

"For we are God's masterpiece. He has created us anew in Christ Jesus, so we can do the good things he planned for us long ago," (Ephesians 2:10 NLT).

*This brief illustration portrays a fictional representation of an imaginary conversation. It's meant to provoke our thinking, using a challenge to search the Holy Scriptures like a Berean scholar, living the charge God assigns from the Bible. God's Word, the Holy Bible, reigns sufficiently. I do not know what Jesus would actually say. My typed words are not divine, certainly. My writing does not carry the weight of the all-powerful and all-sufficient Word of God. Not even close.

Laura Loveberry

Dung Smear

". . . splatter your faces with mature . . ."
Mal. 2:3b NLT

God will smear DUNG on the faces of priests??? Did I read this right? What do I visualize in my daily Scripture reading? How did I miss this part with poop? I try to read through the Bible every year, but I don't recall reading of a fecal face smear!

Studying through the Old Testament, I come to the last book, Malachi. Writers penned the New Testament letters 400 years later. This leads some scholars to reference the space between the Old and New Testament as the "silent years."

I ponder the impact of the last words before this long silence. What profound truths will God share before the lengthy absence of God-breathed writing?

God shares a "dung smear" illustration.

That's right. God includes this verse, *". . . I will smear on your faces the dung of your festival sacrifices . . ."* (Malachi 2:3b NIV).

The context involves the priests failing to honor God and sinning in their sacrifices to the Lord. The application directed towards me remains clear. God hates my sin. To God, my sin disgusts and dishonors like fecal matter smudged on my face.

Can you imagine the stench stuck under the nostrils?

Yech!

Shortly after my reading, I enjoy a glorious hike through the woods. At the end of my wilderness trek, I spot trash along the trail and bend over to clean it up. Leaning, I focus on the rubbish.

Eew!

I nearly pick up with my bare hands, a repulsive feminine product tossed out on the nature trail. Gross! I grasp the word picture. God reteaches me vividly from my morning reading. My sins dishonor, disturb, and downright disgust. My debaucheries look like unexpected garbage on a pleasant path.

Another verse from Psalms pops into my head. *"Wash me thoroughly from mine iniquity, and cleanse me from my sin,"* (Psalm 51:2 KJV). I suggest reading all of

Psalm 51, focusing on the cleansing power of God's forgiveness.

When I do what I know wrongs God, I picture myself walking with a fecal face. Yep. That stinking image helps me halt my sin. I ask forgiveness from God, letting Jesus wash my poopy face clean, metaphorically speaking.

Girl, you can't wash your face clean enough... but God can.

Let's gasp at the sinful mess we sometimes see in our mirror. You and I can confess our depravity, asking God to scrub our face clean with his forgiveness. Let's start our day afresh!

Girl, **LET GOD** wash your face.

Laura Loveberry

The Waiting Room

"I waited and waited and waited for God. At last, he looked; finally, he listened . . ."
Psalm 40:1 MSG

Back in the 70s, someone gives a set of Corvette keys to a sixteen-year-old birthday boy and directs him to look in the garage. He rushes out the door breathless, anticipating his dream car, a 1976 Stingray Corvette.

Everyone knows his desire for the perfect muscle car.

Could his dream be coming true?

The crowd gathers around as the garage door opens and . . . thud! His heart drops to the cold cement floor.

No dream car.

There sits a miniature model car of a Corvette in the middle of the empty garage—a matchbox car of his Vette vision.

The jokes on him.

They cannot afford to give him an actual muscle car. Laughter muffles in the background as his face grows redder.

How could he be so gullible?

Have you ever thought life would deliver your dream, and you were sorely disillusioned? If so, you can relate to this teenager's car disappointment.

Life often brings delays.

Some stall in the waiting room for years.

The Bible refers to long-awaited delays in deeper, more substantial areas than getting hopes dashed for lack of a new automobile.

In the Bible book of Mark, the author writes of a woman seeking solutions for twelve years for her chronic bleeding illness. Not only did this make her sick, but society considered her "unclean" excommunicating her.

She reeks of a stench daily . . . for years.

This humiliation and isolation persist until one day she musters up the courage to move forward through the crowd gathered around Jesus. Her faith in Jesus motivates her even when her illness deprives her of dignity. The woman determines, *"'If only I may touch His clothes, I shall be made well,'"* (Mark 5:28b NKJV).

When Jesus asks who touched him, the long-suffering woman, knowing Jesus healed her instantly, *"fell down before Him and told Him the whole truth. And He said to her, 'Daughter, your faith has made you well . . .'"* (Mark 5:33b-34a NKJV).

Jesus lovingly refers to her as "daughter."

A father cares and loves his child, knowing the hardship they have suffered. Can you imagine how blessed this abandoned woman feels to be called Jesus' daughter?

DAUGHTER!

The living walking LORD cares for her like a father.

In these biblical times, the cultural mores of the society run away, reject, and ridicule her. Not Jesus. Jesus adopts her.

She belongs.

The woman's twelve horrendous years in the waiting room were breaking her, but Jesus makes her whole. Healed!

Jesus can redeem our painful years in the waiting room, too.

Although not written, I envision this daughter of God telling everyone she meets about the transformative power of Jesus. After the long isolation, I speculate she did not waste her pain. I think she used her difficult past to empathize with others, sharing the life-changing power of Jesus Christ.

In the waiting comes painfully gained wisdom, a hard-earned gift from the compassion of God.

Let's return to the sixteen-year-old boy with no actual Corvette, only a matchbox car. He told me his car story over thirty-five years ago.

It stuck with me.

The teen grew into a man, and we married. Mark, my hubster, became a hard-working, self-sacrificing and generous spouse. He never considers spending extravagant money on himself with raising two kids, keeping this family afloat.

Now for the rest of the story.

Mark's birthday is in July. We usually budget $20 for birthday gifts, but I made an exception this year.

Our kids plan an elaborate scavenger hunt, ending in the front of our neighbor's garage. My son films Mark holding a toy corvette clue while reading the attached directions.

Simultaneously, the garage door slowly rolls up.

Mark's dream Corvette sparkles in all its glory.

It's a sparkling blue, 1976 Stingray T-top, complete with an enormous bow and a card with all the names of family and friends pitching in to make this moment possible.

Mark stares at his muscle car. In surreal slow motion, he turns to me, mouth open, eyes huge. Our daughter wraps her arms around his waist. Moving toward Mark, we embrace in a family hug.

> **Sometimes delayed gratification makes the wait worth it.**

Tears flow.

What joy it brings to bless such a well-deserving husband and dad with this auto surprise! Mark's dream car comes with a license plate reading "July 14" to commemorate the memorable celebration he won't soon forget.

Mark beams an ear-to-ear smile.

Have you been in life's waiting room?

We experience heart wrenching delays.

Some broken-hearted barren couples long await a baby. Other people with debilitating illness desperately wait for remission. Many are unemployed, waiting for a job. Some children pray nightly for their parent to come home from a military assignment. Other frustrated singles and married couples wait to embrace a soulmate who will love them for real.

We all sit in a waiting room at one time or another.

Sometimes the despair ends gloriously, like the woman in our Bible story. My husband prioritized his family over a Corvette. He experienced the rewards of delayed gratification by those he values more than his dream car.

Yet, some still wait.

Often, how we choose to live in the waiting determines our life. How we mature, developing wisdom in the waiting room, defines our character. Our quality of living forms by how we choose to grow in the delayed seasons of life.

Let's reach out to God.

Perhaps joining a Bible study or church small group will ease the journey. Maybe ask an authentic Christian to mentor you weekly. We can daily depend on God's Word to fortify us with his power.

Godly character development in the waiting can drive you to a closer authentic relationship with God. God sees—caring for us in the breakdowns, pit stops, and in the waiting, waiting, waiting . . .

Laura Loveberry

Job Application

"The members of the council were amazed when they saw the boldness of Peter and John, for they could see that they were ordinary men with no special training in the Scriptures. They also recognized them as men who had been with Jesus"
Acts 4:13 NLT

What type of job applicant would a CEO choose for a global network designed to influence the entire planet effectively? What if the CEO only selected twelve applicants to universally impact the entire world with an outreach enterprise?

Let's look at an example from 2000 years ago.

Jesus chose a dozen disciples who did not seek the position to train to revolutionize the world forever. CEOs typically select applicants showing proven leadership, platform, or position of prime influence.

Not Jesus.

Jesus selects an unlikely group of men, not the all-stars of management or renowned brilliant minds of the land. Who would choose to initiate a global transforming movement with little-known people on the fringes of society? The world undervalues these folks, judged lowly, but Jesus does not.

Jesus values the "low lives" of civilization.

Remember the woman at the well? In the day's culture, she deemed as the lowest of lows. She represents a mere female gender, according to the women-are-property standards of the day. Humanity depicts her as a despicable Samaritan female referred to as a dredge by public mores, divorced more times than society judges proper.

She's a nothing-of-value non-person.

Jesus breaks the culture norms.

Christ engages in the longest-recorded-in-the-Bible-two-person conversation with this woman. Do you understand the underlining message overturning the cultural stigma of the day? This historically insignificant Samaritan female is NOT invisible to Jesus.

Jesus sees the unseen.

His radical decision to not only see, but acknowledge, actually associating with this woman, challenges the old-school way of doing life. Jesus highly esteems acknowledging the spiritual potential in what the world regards as worthless.

> **Jesus doesn't call the qualified.**
>
> **He qualifies the called.**

Let's revisit the unofficial resumes of our unlikely candidates for world-changing discipleship. We reference fishy-smelling men, a money-extorting tax collector, a rebel, a doubter, unknowns, and the unlikeliest of men to be selected as disciples.

The leader of the worldwide transformation movement rejected prideful, pompous, and popular resumes.

He chose ordinary workers, serving side by side, to go about God's business impacting world history. Jesus hand-picked unknowns for his highly effective and life-altering movement.

Hey, you and I may seize an opportunity here.

Today, Jesus still breaks societal norms by calling us, the unlikely, to join his network of lowly fishermen living for God. We can share the far-reaching love of

Christ. Understand, nobody earns Jesus' love and forgiveness based on self-worth. Jesus offers his love and acceptance to his transforming team of brothers and sisters as a gift to those who believe in him.

By faith in Christ, we join the greatest movement known to humanity. Our unacceptable-to-society-but-acceptable-to-God resume may look as simple as this:

> *"I am a sinner asking God for forgiveness. By faith, I believe Jesus died for my sins and rose from the dead. My trust and faith are in Christ. I believe in Jesus.*
>
> *Signed _____."*

You may be unqualified, noncertified, and unschooled. When summoned by God, we can accept the role by faith, joining the team of Christian ragamuffins. A rewarding, purposeful career, valued by God, awaits those who stride in Jesus' footprints.

The Bible reveals some people, *". . . saw the courage of Peter and John and realized that they were unschooled, ordinary men, they were astonished and they took note that these men had been with Jesus,"* (Acts 4:13 NIV).

Our first job assignment—live in such a manner onlookers will take notice we have been with Jesus.

Gone Amiss

"A time to cry, and I time to laugh."
Eccles. 3:4a NLT

The big day finally arrives.

Representing the state as Mrs. Michigan 2007 thrills me. It's a humbling honor. On the schedule, my family plans to meet the governor at the state capital today. Our special-needs daughter, Madison, swings her feet back and forth in her chair, playing her promised two electronic games. We await our meeting.

We practiced our handshake and good eye-contact manners for weeks before this moment. Our 9-year-old repeated, "Pleased to meet you, Governor."

Since Madison struggles to control herself in new situations, we smile as she remains calm. She is not hyperactively running around the grand hallways, knocking over precious historical statues.

So far, so good.

"Next!" the uniformed guard bellows out. Our turn arrives. Shooting up a quick prayer for this to go well, I grab up our belongings, turning on my camera. Cell phones with cameras became popular later.

Ut! Oh!

The camera battery dies.

Quickly, I snatch the other electronic toy Madison set aside and change out the batteries for my camera. We need to walk in right now. My director requires photos of all events.

Did I mention Madison does not adjust to change of plans well?

Suddenly, Madison yells down the hallway corridor, "Mom, you said I could play with both these toys!" Madison puffs her cheeks, stomping her feet.

She morphs into the meltdown phase.

We cannot soothe her growing irrationalness. I hand my husband the now battery-powered camera. Frantically, we scurry into the prestigious oval office with our family.

The governor greets me by shaking my hand as I introduce my husband, our son, and then I look at our daughter.

My eyebrows raise and eyes widen.

Madison's cheeks puff out with air. Shaking her head, she lowers her frown, squinting her eyes to narrow slits. She jams into unreasonable mode because her promised electronic toy contains no battery. She cannot adjust.

Our weeks of practice fail the test.

Introducing our perturbed child, I say, "This is my daughter, Madison."

Stomping her feet, sticking out her bottom lip, Madison whips her back around to the highest official in the state.

I twitch, sweating profusely. Madison turns defiantly away. Grimacing, my husband whispers sternly out of the side of his mouth, "Madison, say hello to the governor NOW!"

Keeping her feet planted and backside out, Madison cocks her head around frowning, snorting out with sass, "Hi Gov."

Hi Gov?!

She spins her head back around dramatically to the I–am-not-cooperating position, crossing her arms with back to the governor.

Did our daughter royally, with much ado, diss the esteemed position of governor in the historic oval office?!

My brain panics. I bead up, sweating as cameras flash. I envisioned our Mrs. Michigan moment in the revered oval office differently.

Several years pass since this fiasco in the capital. Madison's autism diagnosis helps us understand this hysterical, historical highlight of my queen experience.

Nevertheless, we persist.

Have your best-made plans ever gone berserk?

Reading my favorite book, the Bible, I see how ordinary people like us experience unexpected disruptions. But God extraordinarily works in his divine plans.

Jonah plans a side-trip escape and spends a few desperate days in the slimy stomach of an enormous fish. This fish vomits out the disobedient Jonah, who wipes off the slime to obey God and witness a city repent.

God's mission prevails.

Joe envisions living a dream, but his brothers sell him to slavery. False charges of rape throw him into prison, yet God raises Joseph to the second-most-powerful man in the land.

Then Joseph saves his family from starvation.

Refusing to bow to an idol, Daniel prays on his knees to the one true God. They hurl him into a den of ravenous lions for punishment. God delivers Daniel unscathed to bring God glory! The king changed his view of Daniel's God.

The king made a decree to revere the God of Daniel.

Life tangles and twists.

Our human plans can detour, but God can turn our alternative routes into a reason to celebrate. These memories train us to trust and give God glory.

God is good all the time.

All the time, God is good.

God remains good in our unanticipated and unpredictable life. Always. Our determination to live for God can grow stronger passing through the training course.

Don't dismiss the lessons in this.

Find God's purpose when life goes amiss.

Eventually, Madison ended up cozying up to the governor, who complimented Maddie, suggesting she would make a good governor in the future. I smile.

Laura Loveberry

Hope Rising

"Therefore, we do not lose heart. Though outwardly we are wasting away, yet inwardly we are being renewed day by day."
2 Cor. 4:16 NIV

I heard the statement, "It is what it is. Nothing changes. I am hopeless."

NO! You are NOT without hope.

You can seize hope for the future no matter the sins of your past, no matter your regrets, no matter your inadequacies or the situation holding you down.

You and I can grasp hope in the middle of the hardship.

If you need to rise above your self-made mess and mire, you can climb upward to find purpose beyond your pain. Does our shame and regret keep us down? We can bolster to find hope for our hurt. If you and I fall deep in a pit of despair, we can triumph over this trial.

Grasp God's outstretched hand.

You may reckon you're losing a battle, but God can pull you out of the valley to victory! God can help you trek up your mountain, drop the baggage weighting you down, and guide you to life's ultimate goals.

Deep despair is NOT nothing to God.

Your life matters.

Do you believe this? YOU are ". . . *awesomely and wonderfully made . . .*" (Psalm 139:14b NASB). The *Message Bible* paraphrases these verses with, "*Thank you for making me so wonderfully complex! Your workmanship is marvelous—how well I know it. You watched me as I was being formed in utter seclusion, as I was woven together in the dark of the womb. You saw me before I was born. Every day of my life was recorded in your book. Every moment was laid out before a single day had passed,*" (Psalm 139:13-16 NLT).

God designed you.

God grants purpose to you, right now, even in your season of beyond the hardest of hard. You and I crave a deep desire inside for a genuine relationship with our Creator, a longing to grasp his perspective.

With faith in Jesus Christ, we can come to God asking forgiveness for our failures and for our shame. You and I can wail to God when despondent.

God knows you deeply. He recorded every day of your life before you even lived it. He hears. When you and I cannot do our life, God's compassion does not fail us.

Deep despair is "NOT NOTHING" to God.

NO! It is something!

Despair wrapped around humility looks up to our all-caring, all-knowing God. God reaches down to rescue us in this perfect place of needing him.

Hand Jesus your whole life, your whole heart, your whole stressful situation. Let go and let God. Give all of your man-made aches and pains to the one who created all creation.

God gives do overs, do throughs, do arounds and do up–and-aboves. Trusting in the God of all comfort grants us breakthrough here on earth or above in heaven.

Got God? Then God's got this!

> **Got God? Then you've got this.**

Remember the Bible heroes with mess God used to bless—Daniel in the lion's den, Joseph in a pit, David a murderer and adulterer, Paul the persecutor of believers, Jonah the runaway with a true whale's tale, Rahab the harlot, Noah the ostracized, Esther an orphan and Moses the basket case.

God uses these hopeless situations to inspire us today. Never give up. When God writes your story, it's for his glory. Hope remains for the hopeless. God plots a way out of the deserts, the darkness, and the pits of despair.

Seek God's purposeful plan.

Begin trusting God's higher perspective. We perceive our existence as the backside of a needlepoint drapery with knots, dangling strings, and gnarly chaos of threads.

God sees the topside tapestry.

The underside chaotic process creates our refined masterpiece upside view. God weaves a life pieced together with scraps. Let the Artist finish.

Don't quit.

Our personal hope arises to new heights when we realize God's big picture perspective. Hope holds the Artist's hand, looking up to the Creator.

Laura Loveberry

Impact

"One generation commends your works to another; they tell of your mighty acts."
Psalm 145:4 NIV

Imagine my husband and I wrestling whether or not to stay as church members. The following paragraphs describe two fake stories to illustrate probable consequences.

This fabricated narrative pounds a profound point.

Visualize a fictional scenario with a personal dispute over an injustice taking place at church. Should we stay **or** sprint out, slamming the doors behind, never to return? Leaving the church seems the logical answer for everyone. Is it a quick fix?

Oh, what should we do? What will we do?

***

In the first scenario, we exit the church, never to return. We free ourselves from the glaring eyes and judgement. The relief flows instantly, but temporarily.

The following Sundays, we visit other church services randomly with our wounds and distrust buzzing. We don't allow ourselves to truly connect to other parishioners.

Our angry, disgruntled hearts breed bitterness.

Replaying the injustice in our heads often, our anger oozes until our faces morph into bitter shields. Our children sense our ugly resentment toward the church members. The entire family chooses never to be part of "those hypocrites." Other Sunday-school classmates side with us and leave the church, too.

Years pass. We become desensitize to sin.

We gossip, laughing at the crudest of jokes, living questionable lives where lying and cheating become the norm. We blend into the worldly culture of materialism. Our children lack the growth found in Christian fellowship, Sunday school, and Bible study.

Our kids grow up to marry unbelievers.

Generation after generation live for the moment with no depth of spiritual richness, but we own a lot of "stuff." We mock the Bible-carrying losers. We live without purpose or meaning. The reputation of our family and descendants plummets for the next fifty years.

***

In the second scenario, we pray continually for God's will for this tense situation in our home church. We read the Bible voraciously, seeking his guidance. We choose to stay in this church, praying for restoration.

It's not easy.

Every Sunday the wedge is evident, but we press on at this same church. Our perfect God continues to bless our flawed selves in our not-so-perfect congregation. We forgive those who hurt us and ask for forgiveness from others we hurt. We restore some relationships. Some are not. Our wounds heal. We grow spiritually through the peacemaking process.

Consequences for choices impact generations.

Years pass.

Later, others come to us asking for us to forgive them. We already did, so we smile as God restores more relationships. We apologize for our part of wrong again.

Our children witness our desire to honor God.

They learn to work things out spiritually. We experience personal trials as the church supports our family in crisis. We know first-hand the love of the body of Christ.

We worked through the emotional seasons.

Our adult children transform to devoted believers, staying involved in our church. Our children marry like-minded believers. One of our adult children falls away from church, but church members restore them through their love. Every offspring celebrates joyously the fellowship and community of attending church. They embrace the Bible and living for God.

We live fulfilled for the next fifty years to love God and love broken and restored people . . . just like us.

***

These two fictional stories reveal a powerful truth.

The conclusions are from actual possibilities. We need to pray over decisions and *"Seek the Lord and his strength, seek his face continually,"* (*I Chronicles 16:11 KJV*).

Let's study God's verses for truth in uncertain times. We can understand the lifelong ramifications of our decisions. Choices impact future generations. Some family actions carry long-reaching consequences.

Choose wisely.

Zig and Zag

"What joy for those whose strength comes from the Lord,
who have set their minds on a pilgrimage to Jerusalem."
Psalm 84:5 NLT

Do you remember learning the shortest distance between two points is a straight line?

In life, I discovered the LORD allows the journey between point "A" to "B" to be a zigzag line. Life's unexpected ups and downs sometimes spin round and round.

My years zag and zig.

My zags include the untimely death of my dad and dealing with the "firsts" without him. My first bike ride with my widowed mom brimmed my eyes with tears. How surreal it felt to put my feet on the pedals of Dad's bicycle, knowing his shoes were the last to touch them.

My first summer without both parents camping in the backyard feels unfinished. And I can't imagine how my first Thanksgiving will go without Dad. Who will sit back in the *Lazy Boy* loosening their belt, burping out, "That's a grand dinner!"

I face a year of holidays without my dad.

Other zags are the heart-wrenching issues with my special-needs daughter desperately missing her grandpa. She especially missed his hugs. She struggles to figure out her teen years, to grow socially, and to make wise choices. Grandpa and Madison bonded, understanding each other's temperaments. Even the mention of grandpa's name sends tears flowing down her cheeks.

This year's down-swings include my husband's arthritis flaring up, leaving his body in constant pain. On top of this, I get pink slipped from my teaching position. As I think about missing my students, I am dealing with rejection and financial challenges.

This year's downward dips hurt, but the up-swoops encourage.

The upward zigs include my teaching position returns, and I delight in teaching budding artists again. My son embraces his senior year and flourishes. Cherishing precious time together, Mom and I pray often, encouraging one another. My hubster and I remain soulmates through all the high and low spots on life's pilgrimage.

When I am in the zag waiting for the zig, I draw strength from God. Reading my Bible daily strengthens me. Crying out in the silence and talking out loud to God becomes the norm for me. Embracing a Bible-teaching church starts my week with hope. Blasting worship music uplifts through my days, igniting my praise. I appreciate my friends' support and hugs. Finding my brawn in the Bible, I read.

When life knocks you down, get up & shout, "That all you got?"

"Blessed is the man whose strength is in You, whose heart is set on pilgrimage. As they pass through the Valley . . . They make it a spring; The rain also covers it with pools. They go from

strength to strength . . ." (Psalm 84:5, 6a, 7a NKJV).

Who lives a straight steady line?

No one.

Phooey. Fiddle-faddle. Flappity-flop. Life zigzags. Are you flabbergasted by the crisscross course of your life? I encourage you and I to draw resilience from God as our power source.

> **If your life has no ups & downs, you have flatlined.**

We'll go from strength to strength.

I pray for every person perusing these pages. Maybe some deal with death, job loss, illness, loneliness, prodigal children, financial stress, wrong choices, ruthless consequences or emotional instability. It's skedaddling.

It's skullduggery.

I pray our valley fills with springs and bright blessings abound. I pray God flips our downward zags to upward zigs.

Life zigzags.

It's not a direct line.

Expect to be knocked down. Sometimes you must jump back up shouting, "Is that all you got?!" Then talk to God for wisdom, revitalizing you for the next hill to climb.

The journey is a jagged thingamajig. It's zig zaggy.

Grab God's grit. Don't quit.

Laura Loveberry

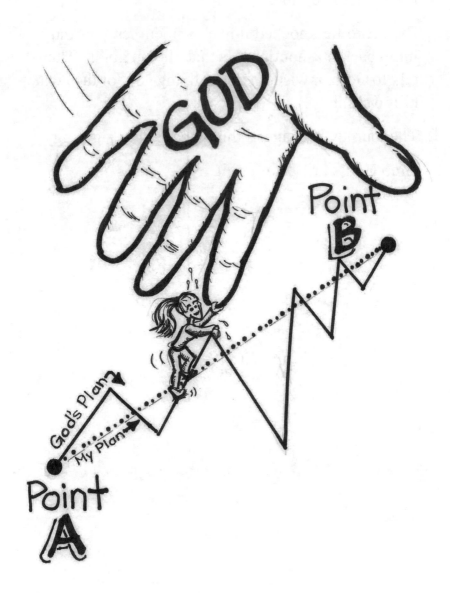

Kiss with a Twist

"Kiss me—full on the mouth!"
Song of Solomon 1:2a MSG

My hubster kisses me goodbye as we scurry to work. Arriving at school, I do my usual crowded hallway weave, walking and greeting many.

Flashing a smile, I say, "Good morning, students!" Unusual glances bounce back. I notice people lingering a little longer, focusing on my face, their eyes smirking.

Grins curl the corner of their mouths.

Nobody actually comments about my face, but their subtle reactions shout, "Yikes! Go look in a mirror." Seeing snickering students, I stride to the restroom to peer at my reflection for a possible problem.

Are you kidding me???

> **How beautiful you are, my darling...**

In the mirror, I spot a white ring of toothpaste circling my mouth. Who can miss it? The toothpaste blares, not to be unnoticed except by my oblivious husband, who kissed me goodbye this morning on these very crusted lips.

How, in the land of lips, can my husband not notice? It's not my makeup. Who can miss the white smudge encircling my mouth? I look sillier than the milk mustache commercials. Got milk?

Egad!

Back home, we discuss this. Maybe I should check the mirror myself before leaving, but he planted a kisseroo on these lips before walking out the door!

Undoubtedly, my school friends still giggle over this.

My hubster answers me as smooth as toothpaste coming out of the tube. Quoting his version of the *Song of Solomon*, he says something like, *"You're so beautiful, my darling, . . . Your smile is generous and full-expressive and strong and clean. Your lips are jewel red, your mouth elegant and inviting, . . . The kisses of your lips are honey, my love, every syllable you speak a delicacy to savor . . .*" (Song of Solomon 4:1a, 3a, 11a MSG).

Mark claims my love so captivated him he noticed nothing amiss at our kiss this morning.

Who can resist passionate flattery?

Head-over-heels, I tumble for his kissable excuse.

His lips pucker. We smooch. I forgive his neglect.

Here is a tip for the inexperienced husbands. Check out this romantic book of the Bible. Perhaps memorize the loving phrases. Maybe the wording, ". . . *thy hair is as a flock of goats . . .*" (Song of Solomon 4:1 KJV), is NOT the most romantic line, but read on. You may discover other tender lines for encouraging your lovely bride.

It could get you off the hook.

Pucker up, readers. The Bible guides in all areas of our lives—even romantic kiss bliss you won't want to miss.

Laura Loveberry

Obstacles to Overcome

"The Lord is the defense of my life; Whom shall I dread?"
Psalm 27:1b NASB

Got zeal?

Do you possess true passion, making a difference in life? If this burning in your heart shines new or different, be prepared for people attempting to squelch it, douse it, or stomp it out completely.

I recommend pursuing your unique desire to bless others, but understand opposition may lurk around the corner.

Even in ministry, folks thwarting your mission may shock you. I recommend pursuing the God-call in your life despite the obstacles.

Obstacles provide opportunities to overcome.

I read about the life of Nehemiah in the Bible. Nehemiah rebuild the crumbled walls around Jerusalem with passion. He motivated, organized, and planned to accomplish this task.

> **We overcome what some meant to destroy us.**

Opposition grew against his rebuilding mission. Workers protected themselves with a weapon in one hand as the other hand lifted the stones for the wall.

They built amid threats, adversity, and mocking. They prayerfully completed the task for the glory of God. This shows fortitude.

We need this resilience.

Studying Nehemiah, I recalled barriers in ministry I faced. My unique sign-language drama set to music got banned in some places. Leadership suggested I should focus on children's church instead of my current speaking ministry to women. Production cost for CDs, DVDs, and books seemed too costly a financial undertaking. My techy skills were lacking, and I accidentally deleted a book nearly completed. Gone.

These challenges loomed like a mountain.

Years passed since I first stepped up to the platform with shaky knees and sweaty palms. My heart's desire remains to touch the lives of seekers, to share the life-changing power of Jesus Christ, and to inspire people to build spiritual muscle.

God moved mountains in ministry.

I now minister at a church once banning my signing. I enjoy a full speaking schedule, write for three magazines, earned a doctorate in ministry, and offer encouraging books and DVDs to uplift.

God helping us, you and I can persevere.

Previously, my crumbing heart collapsed.

Brick by brick, the LORD can build us back up through his Holy Spirit. Bible study groups, Christian friends, circumstances, church, personal Bible reading, and a supportive family can help us seek God's guidance.

How about it?

Are you and I walking toward our destiny?

Are you? Are you and I living out our passion?

It's difficult. Nehemiah offers encouragement, saying, ". . . *But now, God, strengthen my hands.*" (Nehemiah 6:9b NASB) and ". . . *the joy of the LORD is your refuge,*" (Nehemiah 8:10b NASB).

Don't resign before your time.

I implore us to never give up pursuing our purpose-driven life. Let's use our gifts to live intentionally building up others, glorifying God. Read the book of Nehemiah.

Build a worthy life.

Will we follow our calling no matter what stones block our way?

Our obstacles provide opportunities to overcome.

Mire to Choir

"He lifted me out of the ditch, pulled me from deep mud.
He stood me up on a solid rock to make sure I wouldn't
slip."
Psalm 40:2 MSG

Have you ever slipped into the mud and mire? I am talking about over-the-nose deep in a sloshy slimy pit.

One summer, working as assistant to my brother, the land surveyor, he suggests we walk all the way around the field. The trench with stagnant water may be deeper than it appears.

Carrying a forty-pound surveyor tripod on my shoulders, I do not want to trudge a single step further than necessary. Let's get this summer job done, taking the short-cut through the ditch.

My brother warns me some farm ditches appear shallow, but are much deeper than expected.

I take the chance.

Balancing the cumbersome tripod on my shoulders, I leap halfway across the stench trench. My boots sink. Muddy silt rushes inside. I struggle to move another step.

Hullabaloo!

I sink waist deep in cow doo doo!

I slosh chest-deep, holding up the heavy equipment over my head. My brother rescues the expensive tripod with little regard for his sinking sis.

I'm a stranded nincompoop!

After saving the all-important tripod, my bro's laughing fit subsides, eventually. He extends the surveyor measuring rod toward me. I grasp the pole, struggle my way out of the slimy ditch and burst into a hallelujah chorus.

"Hallelujah!"

Dramatically, I sing out in *Handel's Messiah* style for full effect. I stand drenched and dripping in the scum juice of liquefied cow dung.

Discombobulated, we tumble into life's sinkholes.

Reminding me of a biblical metaphor, the Psalms offer help for crawling out of the depths of drudgery, *"I waited patiently for the LORD; he turned to me and heard my cry. He lifted me out of the slimy pit, out of the mud and mire; he set my feet on a rock and gave me a firm place to stand. He put a new song in my mouth, a hymn of praise to our God . . ."* (Psalm 40:1-3a NIV).

The Lord is a ladder for climbing out of your pit.

I quote this "go to" verse when needing a sure footing. Often, I repeat these verses, renewing my mind on the slippery slopes of life. These scriptures offer solid ground to stand when everything goes amuck!

Never concede defeat in the muck of misery.

Crawl your way up and out of your season of sludge. I encourage reciting the lyrics of Psalm 40 penned as a song to be sung repeatedly.

You and I can sing the HALLELUJAH-style chorus going from mire to choir!

Laura Loveberry

Oh SNAP

"Pray without ceasing,"
1 Thes. 5:17 KJV

Oh, SNAP!

A woman from the audience talks calmly with me after my keynote speaking event. This gal battles the war of her life—stage 4 cancer. Her situation overwhelms my human thinking.

I cannot wrap my mind around her dire state.

Listening, I contemplate advice to give. What encouragement can I offer? Recalling from my past clumsy mistakes, my awkward advice often fails. Who needs it?

Prayer trumps advice.

We grow spiritually when we take our rough trials straight to our all-seeing, all-knowing, and all-feeling

God. The acronym I call on in times where no words work is "Oh, S.N.A.P!"

It stands for, "Oh, STOP NOW AND PRAY!"

It's all I got.

Amid the high energy surrounding us, women wait to chat. I place my hand on her shoulder. We talk aloud to our all-powerful God.

Oh, we "stop now and pray" in the name of Jesus.

Hearing us pray, others join in laying hands on her shoulders, talking to God on her behalf.

Time holds still.

Wiping our prayer tears, we hug, then carry on with the responsibilities of the planned day.

Years later, and hundreds of speaking occasions in between, I attend an event when a gal seeks me out. Meeting so many women in ministry, I do not recognize her.

She shares her story of remission after being diagnosed with stage 4 cancer. Spontaneously, I jump at the opportunity to pray with her, praising God for the miracle.

Oh. S.N.A.P..

With tears flowing, she says, "That's exactly what you did with me years ago at a ladies' retreat. You asked to pray with me. Cancer filled me back then."

This woman lives with side effects from chemo and treatments, but she beats the medical odds. She lives in remission! What a blessing beyond words, giving all glory to God!

This inspires me to continue to "SNAP" when approached with mega unfixable problems. We do not possess the human power to solve all life's problems instantly, but with an "Oh SNAP" response, we hand it over to our God. He can heal. Some believers receive full healing in heaven—other people experience healing on earth.

Oh! S.N.A.P.
STOP
NOW
AND
PRAY

Both bring praise to God.

When we chat with a person in the middle of a mess beyond comprehension, I encourage us to STOP NOW AND PRAY with them. We can do this in the grocery store, in the parking lot, in the church hallway, at the workplace, on the sports field, in a Facebook message, or on the phone.

God calls us to join his mission.

Let's "SNAP" to it, even with the hustle and bustle around us. We can bring in the calm, taking it to the God who hears.

I do not pretend to understand who grabs healing here and who finds wholeness in heaven. But we can trust God above to help us throughout our journey from here to there.

"Praise be to the God and Father of our Lord Jesus Christ, the Father of compassion and the God of all comfort," (2 Cor. 1:3 NIV).

Zeal Deal

*"We cannot stop telling about the wonderful things we saw
Jesus do and heard him say."*
Acts 4:20 TLB

Have you met a person with a distinct passion?

Could you identify their strong passion within a few minutes of meeting them?

Maybe you get an invitation to a party, the host motivated by a multi-marketing plan designed to build her career. Some people believe in the product they offer, making it a top priority. They passionately promote it in conversation and constant social media posts.

They got zeal for their deal.

People need to make a living. I certainly appreciate folks working hard to support their family. But, as a follower of Christ, this gives me pause. I reflect on myself.

As a Christian, am I as passionate about sharing Jesus?

Jesus rocks as the ultimate life-changer!

Knowing Jesus intimately offers a person peace, purpose, and the promise of life forever with God. Followers of Christ know Jesus gives strength-for–the-journey, power-for-the-hour, and purpose for living.

Shouldn't Christians serve as sold-out ambassadors?

Why are we not as passionate about offering Jesus to all we meet? Why?

I ask this question to myself and other believers. We know the real deal of a lifetime. Yet these marketing people sometimes share their program more than we share God's plan for true spiritual renewal.

Conviction hits me.

Marketers go to more meetings, to get more motivation, to sell more "stuff." More. More. More. They set goals and go for it. Networkers offer to "raise our standard of living."

As believers, we experience the unconditional, forgiving, life-springing love of God. Why can't we pray each day for God to open the doors for us to clearly, lovingly, and joyfully share our passion in life to LOVE GOD and LOVE PEOPLE? If we truly love people, won't we stand ready to share our faith as God clearly directs our paths?

I pray our lives reflect God, so others will ask what gives our life peace and purpose. I pray for boldness sharing our passion, witnessing God working in the hearts of seekers.

I challenge myself and others to be like Peter and John. They, when asked not to talk about Jesus, replied, *"As for us, we cannot help speaking about what we have seen and heard,"* (Acts 4:20 NIV).

Peter and John met the living, risen-from-the-dead Jesus. They sold out for the cause. The Holy Spirit filled them, and they spoke of the life-altering power of knowing Jesus.

Our God's not dead.

Modern-day believers still talk to Jesus often through prayer and Bible study. We testify to the power of Christ to change lives. We hear stories of family and friends repenting, reforming and rescued from a life without hope.

If we possess passion and purpose, shouldn't it be for spreading the love of God?! We can know Jesus intimately through his Word. Shouldn't we live in such a way we cannot help speaking about what we saw and heard?

We can study the book of Acts in the Bible again.

Whoosh! I'm talking about fear-facing fervor for God.

These ordinary, uneducated, persecuted people spoke powerfully for Jesus. The Holy Spirit motivated movement. Let's be bold! Let's talk about what we have seen and heard in the name of Jesus!

Let our zeal be for real. SPEAK UP!

Rahab's Rehab

"For the LORD your God is the supreme God of the heavens above and the earth below."
Joshua 2:11b NLT

Are you haunted by past failure?

Our past does not need to be our future. Period. We can learn from our hopeless failures. We can experience a life lesson that grows into a hope-filled future.

A bright inspiration shines forth out of the darkness.

My favorite people have histories filled with failures, horrendous sins, and ungodly mistakes.

I fail majorly, messily, and miserably. My "sistas-in-Christ" and bestie friends fell on their journey, too. God's recovery power in me and my down-to-earth friends grows our faith in the God of heaven.

Our burdens no longer bury us.

Look at a woman in scripture from over 3000 years ago. Rahab is a heroine of the faith in the classic bestselling book. Rahab, the harlot, a common prostitute living in a humble dwelling on the wall of Jericho, grabs honor as one of two women in the remarkable Hebrew chapter eleven. Many consider this the spiritual Hall of Fame chapter of the Bible.

A former hooker lands her name in the hall of fame.

When Joshua sends two spies to check out the city of Jericho, God allows these scouts to meet Rahab. God grabs Rahab's heart as evidence of her referring to the LORD by his personal name, YAHWEH. This indicates Rahab's newfound belief in the living God.

The citizens of Jericho shake in their sandals with the news of Israel's army and their mighty power. But Rahab bravely puts her faith in the God of heaven and earth, so she hides the Israelite spies.

She plans their getaway.

Rahab, living on the edge of society near the city wall, helps the spies escape. In return, a red cord marks her home to prevent any harm to her household by the invading Israelites.

Significantly, the red cord symbolizes Jesus' sacrifice for our sins, saving believers from death, too. Displaying the blood-red cord protected Rahab.

The representative blood-red cord saves her.

Despite her own scandalous occupation, Rahab determines the Israelite God to be worthy of trust. Our harlot hero is far from perfect, a liar, and a sexual sinner who came to God with a sordid past.

> **Don't be a prisoner of your past. Jesus is the key to set you free.**

Some might distance from her.

But our God draws close. God, seeing beyond the ugly prostitution, recognizes her beautiful heart. Rahab confirms her faith in God, who delivers her out of her dilemma.

"It was by faith that Rahab the prostitute was not destroyed with the people in her city who refused to obey God. For she had given a friendly welcome to the spies . . . " (Hebrews 11:31 NLT).

Are we haunted by our past?

Do we feel shame, marked with a scarlet letter? Does it define us still today? Do we fall into a sinful habit of losing all hope? Are we unworthy and ashamed?

Look how our heroine's story ends.

Later, Rahab bore a son named Boaz. He lived righteously as a kinsman redeemer for Ruth. Not put off by her race, he honored Ruth with kindness and a dramatic wedding proposal. Boaz rocks the "righteous man" title despite his mom's former occupation. Rahab's conversion led her to raise a godly son into manhood.

Future generations benefitted by her fearless faith.

Rahab's story doesn't stop there.

God does not distance himself, but comes nearer. Rahab shines as one of two women honored in the heroes of the faith book of the Bible.

She weaves into the ancestry of Jesus Christ.

Do you and I get the impact of this last statement? She links in the line of Jesus, the Savior of the world! Rahab is one of Jesus' great-grandmothers.

Jesus descends from Rahab.

Faith changes everything.

Is our past laden with deceit, sin, or hopelessness? Have you failed miserably, like me and my besties? Maybe our haunting sins differ, but you and I need the same forgiveness. Our crooked sins, God can set straight.

Come as you are.

I did.

Place your faith in the God of Rahab, the God of heaven and earth. He longs to use us in his kingdom's work. You and I hold value, no matter our past.

Do not allow our past to hold us fast.

Step forward with the courage of Rahab.

Perfection does not mark faith-filled believers, but we know the engraved hands of Jesus. He lifts our sinful burden, washes us clean, setting us free. Our past merely reminds us of God's present-day power to change our wrong direction, solve our dire situations, and redirect our destiny.

Rahab's disgraceful past belongs in the Bible. You and I can relate. I'm a selfish, self-centered, and so controlling sinner needing a Savior. If God uses a former prostitute, then God, by his grace, can use forgiven sinners with true faith in Jesus.

Our past remains our past.

Do you need to forge forward with the courage of Rahab? You can ask one of those big-Bible-reading authentic Christians you know, "Can you explain faith in Jesus Christ?"

No matter how shameful our history, our courage to inquire matters. Placing our faith in the God of the Israelites can transform everything.

The whole shebang changes.

You are the "whosoever" in this life-altering Bible verse. *"For God so loved the world, that he gave his only begotten Son, that **whosoever** believeth in him should not perish, but have everlasting life,"* (John 3:16 KJV).

Jesus can "Rahabize" everyone, even you and I. Yes, I made up that word. Rahab's rehab inspires our renewal.

If we resemble Rahab, we can rehab!

Dance of Romance

"My beloved spoke and said to me, 'Arise my darling, my beautiful one, and come with me."
Song of Solomon 2:10a NIV

Do you want a romantic man?

Am I a marriage expert? Malarkey! But my hubster, Mark rocks as the love of my life. We celebrate almost 40 years of marriage.

Isn't it wise to reveal to my husband just what softens my woman's heart the most? I dislike the hard-to-get approach. I love the hard-to-forget tactic. Here's an unforgettable romance from my feminine perspective.

I spell this out to my hubster.

I soften when my husband enters the room, touching my face, gently kissing me on the forehead, whispering sweetly, snuggling up to my ear, "I love you, my queen."

Puddled.

It does not take much for my man to melt me when this happens. I mush just thinking about it. Also, taking my hand for a dance spin, dipping me in the kitchen as he passes by delights me.

> **Forehead kisses melt her heart.**

I remember hearing about a husband who worked in a factory for years. Every single day, no matter how exhausted, he tracked down his cherished wife after opening the door. He takes both of her hands in his, kissing her hard-working hands softly on each knuckle.

He says tenderly, "I love these beautiful, beautiful hands." Daily, he caresses and kisses her hands, pronouncing, "I love my bride. It's good to be home."

Every. Single. Day.

Do you think she felt appreciated and loved for over fifty years? Oh, yeah!

How about those romantic glances from across the room when no one else notices? Just mouthing the words, "I love you," hits like a 12 on the 1-10 scale. Knowing even in a crowd, his mind focuses on me, confirms "us."

Gentle squeezes to my hand and timely winks ignite sensibilities I cherish, too.

Here's another helpful hint. Husbands often forget to let the wife walk in front when an aisle narrows. My husband sometimes overlooks this until I touch his sleeve, nudging him back to me discreetly. We smile as he places his hand on the small of my back, guiding me on as I walk in front of him.

In restaurants, I see the man awkwardly walking ahead of his date. Cringe. This dishonors the woman. We still work on this. My husband mostly remembers cherishing me every single step. We make strides in this area, demonstrating public manners for each other.

"Love is kind."

Another biblical characteristic can be the sweet song of your marriage every day. Drop the negative tone, the tit-for-tat, underlying mean digs, grabbing the last word, needing to be right, snarky undertone, and less-than-honoring ways.

Stop it.

The Bible book, *Song of Solomon*, overflows with passionate words

> **My happy place is inside your hug.**

of communicating love and romance. Read it. Take action and communicate in love with thoughtfulness and sensible timing. Kind words with thoughtful delivery make a wife feel quintessentially feminine.

Whisper to her.

When a woman feels cherished in her love language, she wants to express love in return. When you act like her knight, she respects your manliness.

Women long for love like men need respect.

Read these divine and romantic words this biblical couple use with each other in the *Song of Solomon*. I especially love the phrase, *". . . I found him whom my soul loveth . . ."* (Song of Solomon 3:4 KJV).

Talk to your wife about your need for respect.

Be the leader worthy of her admiration.

The biblical marriage commitment, *"My beloved is mine, and I am his,"* (Sol 2:16 NASB), allows a woman the sense of security, holding her husband's undivided heart. She can give herself fully to the relationship without holding back.

Reciprocal kindheartedness creates soulmates.

Prioritize each other. Be genuine. Make your happy place a wraparound hug. Soulmates delight with less fight. It's a win/win for the husband and wife and the romantic life!

Focus on the things she does well, celebrating them. A wife, feeling appreciated, will often want to do more than expected. It goes both ways.

How about praying together and the husband initiate it?

If a struggle or hardship arises, if a colossal decision needs to be made, if you find yourselves out of sync with each other; then take her by the hand offering, to pray out loud with her about the issue.

If a disagreement comes when you need to leave for work, assure her you love her forever and will resolve it when you return. Admit you're upset, but let her know it will be okay. State that your commitment is permanent.

Be forgiving.

In the book of Romans, it reads, *"Be joyful in hope, patient in affliction, faithful in prayer,"* (Rom 12:12 NIV).

You can even start a habit of praying together before you fall asleep or prior to leaving for work. Daily, my hubster prays with me before stepping out the door in the morning.

It shows spiritual leadership.

Thank God for your blessings together.

Women like hearing, "I love you." If a wife takes effort to slightly improving her appearance, please encourage her with, "You look beautiful." Most women love signs of affection in public. Reach over. Hold her hand. At the restaurant, look up at her more than down at your plate. For women, dining embraces the relational opportunity more than the food served.

Men like hearing, "Thank you. I appreciate you. Good job!" Men want to know their wife desires them. Side by side companionship while my hubster works on a project can encourage, as long as I don't tell him how to do it better the entire time. *Wink.*

Wives should vocalize their gratitude for their husband's daily working and providing. It's a manhood issue.

And happy couples say "thank you" often.

Happily married people thank their spouse verbally for every simple gesture all day long, looking for ways to express appreciation.

We can treat our spouse like a best friend.

We can shoot text messages to our mate during the day or call and leave short words of encouragement on their voice mail. We can schedule times to just engage in talking together.

Plan it. Prioritize each other. Communicate more positively than negatively. Nobody needs a dripping faucet of disapproval.

These few tips may help transform relationships.

My best advice involves becoming a man who reads and applies the Word of God, allowing God to develop your character. It transforms.

Reading the book, *The 5 Love Languages* by Gary Chapman, may you help understand your spouse better. Study your mate. Does your spouse appreciate words, touch, gifts, service, or time? Find out. Being a loving partner, growing spiritually and relationally, takes intentional effort.

Wives can be high maintenance.

I know. I am one.

Wives can do our part to bless the marriage by demonstrating respect for our spouse. The book by Emerson Eggerichs, *Love and Respect,* helped me recognize the areas I needed to renovate.

I fall short with my bossiness. I sometime nag, but when I daily absorb the Scriptures, my heart softens to my husband's leadership. Then escaping to the corner of the roof doesn't sound like a better option for my hubster.

Ballroom dancing is a metaphor for marriage.

We know. We took ballroom dancing lessons. He did this for me. I needed to let him lead and not count out loud directing him. When I yield to his loving lead, we flow together on the dance floor.

Dancing lessons helped our marriage.

It's true.

We still take lessons. He's "Da Man" when we swing on the dance floor. It's fun for both of us. Men leading with love in the dance of marriage can twirl their girl, making her heart swirl. Remember, our kitchens make a delectable place for dancing and romancing, along with spicing up our meals.

Tada!

These are my tips to keep locking lips.

Goodbye Chaos Hello Calm

Laura Loveberry

Balm for Calm

"God will fight the battle for you. And you? You keep your mouths shut!"
Exodus 14:14 MSG

Have your dreams ever dashed down to disaster? You may have wanted the best job, a fairytale marriage, perfect children, and a lifetime of happiness and a good health.

KABOOM!

Sometimes life blows up, dropping unexpected events, turning our plans upside down. We need to adjust to the topsy-turvy, drawing steady strength from a source beyond ourself and carry on.

As the Brits say, we need to "Stay strong and carry on." The teacher says, "Stay strong and pretend it is in the lesson plan." And "Stay calm and remind oneself summer's almost here." As the boater says, "Stay calm and stay anchored."

Many readers think, "Stay calm and put on fuzzy PJs." "Stay calm and eat a cupcake." "Stay calm, kids will be in bed soon." As the models in magazines may say, "Stay calm and buy stilettos." I tried all of this plus, "Stay calm and eat chocolate." "Stay calm and call your bestie friend." And "Stay calm and cry in the shower."

Staying calm during chaos remains possible if we hold a sliver of hope. When we derail off Plan A, remember the alphabet contains 26 letters for our options to recover. The tough part occurs when plummeting to Plan Z.

Then what?

The Lord told Moses, *"The Lord himself will fight for you. Just stay calm."* (Exodus 14:14 NLT). Whoa! Think about it. Before all these saying began popping up everywhere, God spoke it. It's outstanding knowing God stands available for calming power to prevail!

This God-breathed timeless advice helped Moses in the trenches. God's Word can inspire us today. Let's remember, "Just stay calm," because God remains in control. When surrounded with no escape, God makes a way if HE chooses.

With gut level gratitude, I state God can make a way through my trembling trail when it appears impossible to travail. When humanly I can't, God can.

> **Stay calm and call on God.**

In this life, we can live out our destiny. We secure the source of strength just a conversation with God away.

He's our balm to stay calm.

God stands as a father to the fatherless, a friend to the end, our shelter in the storm, our comforter, wonderful counselor, and the great I AM.

"Stay calm . . . and call on God."

Laura Loveberry

Power of B-U-T

*"But the Lord stood at my side and
gave me strength . . ."*
2 Tim. 4:17a NIV

Do you possess a powerful calling, passion, or purpose in your life, yet progress seems postponed? Have faltering economics, forceful opposition, or failing support from friends and family seemed to throw a wrench into your plans?

Do you desire to live out your dream, but your destiny dies?

I stumble upon a paragraph in my daily Bible reading journey, and BAM, inspiration BOOMS off the page, igniting my heart.

God chose David to be king, then he waited years while jealous Saul tried to kill him. Family opposed David's heart calling. His closest comrades turned against him, threatening to stone him to death.

"When David and his men reached Ziklag, they found it destroyed by fire and their wives and sons and daughters taken captive. So David and his men wept aloud until they had no strength left to weep. . .. David was greatly distressed because the men were talking of stoning him; each one was bitter in spirit because of his sons and daughters. But David found strength in the Lord his God," (1 Samuel 30:3-6 NIV).

Hello!

When they challenge our calling, remember the zigzag in Ziklag. The world pounded down on David, the man after God's own heart. David revives himself in the LORD. He encourages himself with our all-powerful God, finding strength to carry on.

You can stay calm and carry on with God's might.

It's like blah, blah, blah . . .*"BUT"* we can find strength in the LORD our God. Don't you just love the *"BUT"*s in the Bible? The word *"but"* signifies the change of outlook. Before the *"but"* moment, things appear hopeless then . . . BING! BONG! BOOM! *BUT!*

BUT God can ignite the hope.

BUT God can spark up the exhausted.

BUT God can fan the flame.

> **I don't get this, BUT God, YOU got this.**

These *BUT* moments in life turn our trials into triumph. We get up off the ground, grasping God. You and I can seize the power in our Bible hour. We got God, and God's got this.

Grab this tiny three-letter word B-U-T. Change our course of dismay, disappointment, and delay. We can turn on our G-O-D way!

Badda BAM! Badda BOOM! Badda *BUT!*

Laura Loveberry

The Answer "No"

"We are hard pressed on every side, but not crushed; perplexed, but not in despair; persecuted, but not abandoned; struck down, but not destroyed."
2 Cor. 4:8-9 NIV

Not ALL asking, begging, pleading, crying out in the dark, brings instant healing. Nope. Some problems remain unsolved. Not all relationships get fixed. Some wounds don't heal.

Many prayers receive answers immediately. My lump—not cancer. My husband's mass—not terminal. Many prayers get the answer we want.

Praise God!

Some answers don't align with our desires.

Can we still praise God when the answer resounds with a loud "NO?" How do we react when our deepest, most crucial hopes fall below our expectations?

Does our all-knowing and all-powerful God of the universe care? What happens when God does not live up to our plans? Our human hopes do not always land on the same plane as the God of the past, present, and future.

Ponder on this Bible verse. *"And blessed is he who does not take offense at Me."* (Matthew 11:6 NASB). Do we get this? The capitalized "Me" refers to God. Are you and I resentfully affronted by God's design of our life?

Do we get mad at God's all-encompassing will?

Some things do NOT go by our miniscule plans.

God creates a gigantic glorious overall eternity for those with faith in Jesus. Who are we to direct the one True God? He places the stars in the sky and tells the sun when to rise. God runs the earth's details.

I encourage you not to turn *from* God in monumental disappointment, but to love God turning *toward* him. Seek God through the hardest seasons. Keep focusing on ways God blesses you and me in the shattered place.

Wrecked people can restore, rebuilt, and redesign themselves. They can grow in compassion, increase in empathy, and gain an understanding of others.

Empathic people touch humanity in trauma.

You and I can pull away from God, living a bitter, disillusioned life. We can blame God for not doing what we judge best. Or we can choose NOT to be ugly and cynical against God's ways, accepting the life God lays out for us.

This pivot point determines the rest of our life. You and I can live for God in peace beyond all human understanding.

You determine your comeback.

Are we wiser than God?

I am not.

God allows challenges in our lives.

Some of our prayers receive the deeply painful answer, "NO." I don't do "no" well, but I am working on my response of receiving "Thy will be done." We can say this out loud as we talk to God in our need, "God's will be done."

God's will should be our stance on struggles. My response eventually lands there, but I wobble sometimes in trusting God entirely and without stalling.

**You are God.
I am not.**

Delayed trust signals distrust.

Wailing desperate prayers to God, the answer imploded the opposite of my request. My womb remains barren.

"Thy will be done."

The doctor's office misplaced my dad's medical file, resulting in delayed treatment and my dad dying of cancer.

"Thy will be done."

My once athletic husband lives in silent chronic arthritic pain.

"Thy will be done."

Although dramatically improving, autism issues still upset the calm in our family.

"Thy will be done."

You and I are not quitters.

Disappointments are real. But they're not real estate. We don't need to live there.

Even when numb, lost in the loss, you and I do not quit. Our hands may tremble, our throat tightens, and our mind replays the tragic moment. Yet we never give up. We turn to God for strength. We pray to God over these trials, striving toward peace in the hardest of everyday living.

But when the answer hits with loss of a deeply loved life, loss of a lifetime dream, or loss so deep it crushes us, then we must decide how to inch, crawl, and drag forward.

The biblical wisdom for our brokenness accepts "Thy will be done." We can stop the "if only" thoughts and live in the new normal, the different, and the forever-changed life God allowed.

We can gradually, grieving and growing, take our next gasp toward rejuvenating, renewing and rejoicing in the God of all comfort.

Breathe in deeply and exhale slowly.

We can journey back to joy. When the "but if not" happens, and it does not deliver us as we pleaded, we can continue to honor God as holy.

We can accept what we cannot change.

Tears roll down our face. We fill our lungs with air and slowly blow out. We will trust through these trials.

When "No" says "Hello" we know where to go. We lift our eyes up to heaven with hands clutching our heart. His kingdom will come.

THY WILL BE DONE.

Laura Loveberry

Stop Fish Go Fish

"Many are the plans in a person's heart, but it is the
Lord's purpose that prevails."
Prov. 19:21 NIV

The exhausted fishermen grumble. They threw their fish nets all night. Not one fish did they drag in. The fisherman, hunching over, slowly row to the shore.

Nothing.

Have you experienced a time when nothing seemed to go right and you collapse, bushed? These salty men slump in the same boat. They are sweaty from the draining work. Grimy and filthy, they row back with empty nets.

While cleaning up the nets, a multitude of people hurry by, seeking a certain rabbi named Jesus. The crowd pushes close to Jesus, near the shoreline. Cleaning their nets, the fisherman glance up.

Jesus asks to climb into Simon's boat. He asks the fatigued fisherman to launch out so he could speak from off shore. Hunched over, Simon puffs out an obliging sigh.

Jesus addresses the crowd from on the boat.

Imagine the front row, where Simon sat listening to the words of Jesus penetrating deep into his weary body. After Simon hears the man of God, he perks up. Then Jesus asks Simon to launch out to the deep, dropping the net.

Does Simon roll his eyes and exhale deeply?

Can you visualize Simon, so moved hearing Jesus speak, yet so exhausted after fishing all night? Now this carpenter/teacher, Jesus, gives Simon, the seasoned fisherman, advice on where to drop the net.

I can almost hear Simon clearing his throat, answering, *"Master, we have toiled all night and caught nothing: nevertheless, at thy word I will let down the net,"* (Luke 5:5b KJV).

Would Simon shake his head? Does Simon's body language signal to Jesus that the fish will not be caught? Simon obeys nevertheless.

He throws the net, spreading it along the water.

Suddenly, the fishermen's eyes bulge open. Their muscles strain at the weight of the nets. Laughter and robust voices burst from the previously dog-tired crew.

An overflowing boatload of fish swim into the net.

The wide-eyed, roaring fisherman signals for his partner's boat to help with the nets bursting from the load. Their boats nearly sink from the weight of the fish!

This comes about after exhausted Simon quits fishing, hears the Godman speak, and then witnesses Jesus make the fish obey and fill their nets.

Simon witnesses two miracles!

God prevents every fish from swimming into the net at night. Did God stop the fish all night? I think so. Consider this. Jesus uses the frustrating all-night struggle to awaken Simon's soul for the next day. Jesus makes these same fish that avoided the net, now flow right into their nets at daylight.

It demonstrates to Simon the authority of Jesus.

After Simon's dismal evening, he witnessed a miracle. Jesus sent the fish.

Even the fish obey Jesus.

God's miracles include allowing us to go through dreary, exhausting times. Then we see the full impact of the power of God to change our dismal circumstances.

Often miracles flow after distress primes us.

Understanding these two miracles, of keeping fish out, and then guiding fish in, both point to the power of Jesus.

The bad time set up the good time.

Together, both miracles lead Simon to give up his fishing career to follow the Godman who spoke from his boat.

When Simon saw it, he fell at Jesus' knees begging him to depart from him, knowing Jesus knew Simon was an unworthy, sinful man. Jesus said to him, *"Do not be afraid. From now on you will catch men."* (Luke 5:10 NKJV).

God stopped the fish.

> **Your hard chapter sets up a story for God's glory.**

Do you see the miserable miracle of no fish as a setup for God's mighty miracle of overflowing fish nets to convert a fisherman to a fisher of men?

Has God allowed a miracle of a dismal, draining night to set you up to experience how God's power can change dark nights to dramatic morning delights?

Simon relates to God's word picture. It's no fish tale. It's the metaphor of Simon's life. Simon identifies with the word picture to be a fisher of men. A fisherman.

Often, God allows hardship so we can testify to God's power for the miraculous.

Folks in the same boat as us need to know of the overcoming power of God. We, like Simon Peter, can become a fisher of men when we give God the glory, telling our story.

Often, God comes through for us after a night of despair.

We, too, can be fishers of men!

Laura Loveberry

Peace in the Storm

"Peace I leave with you, My peace I give to you; not as the world gives do I give to you. Let not your heart be troubled neither let it be afraid."
John 14:27 NKJV

In the book of Philippines, Paul explains, *"Rejoice in the Lord always. I will say it again: Rejoice! Let your gentleness be evident to all. The Lord is near. Do not be anxious about anything, but in every situation, by prayer and petition, with thanksgiving, present your requests to God. And the peace of God, which transcends all understanding, will guard your hearts and your minds in Christ Jesus,"* (Phil. 4:4-7 NIV).

We witnessed the middle of a storm when visiting my parents. After hours jam-packed in the family car, my entire family, plus my son's steady girlfriend, arrived in Florida.

But this is not the usual fun-in-the-sun trip.

My Dad faces a threatening storm on the horizon. Cancer. Just the word evokes a tempest fear of hurricane proportions.

Will this be the last trip to see our family patriarch?

Our visit allows us to witness a cancer-filled man at peace in the eye of the storm. Dad's days seem numbered, yet he does not need to make a bucket list. He lived his life full, placed his faith in Jesus recently, and experiences perfect peace.

Most of his time is in the dad recliner in the living room. For our visit, Dad reserves up his energy to take us all out on the boat to our favorite little island beach. We call it Disappearing Island. The ocean tides never keep the sand the same and sections fade underwater in high tide.

Ironically, the island shrunk to the smallest size in years. Dad stays on the boat enjoying watching his granddaughter on the shore catch minnows with her pink fishing net. My dad laughs at our silly seagull chasing and smiles during his last day "beaching" with family.

Boating back to their house, my brothers and sister join for a last reunion. We celebrate life sitting around the table with a home-cooked meal, laughing and sharing family stories.

Catching up on our lives, my siblings giggle in the reminiscing. Dad smiles, gazing around the table. He grins, nodding his head in satisfaction, knowing his kids will carry onward.

Yet, looming in the room, the ever-present weight of Dad's cancer burdens our hearts. The diagnosis— terminal.

Our outward party enjoys every moment.

Our inward hearts grieve.

It's time for our final goodbye.

Dad grimaces, shuffling out to the car to say goodbyes. Emotions float to the surface knowing this might be the last we stand all together. Our eyes brim with water. Talking feels awkward.

There are no adequate words.

I announce, "Group hug!" Interlocking our arms over shoulders, we form a circle in the driveway. Prompted to pray, we bow our heads in the circle. I thank God for our time together with Mom and Dad.

My voice cracks.

I stop talking, gasping for a deep breath.

Our teenage son fills in the gap, taking over in prayer. Next, my daughter sweetly talks to God. Right around the circle, we share spontaneous prayers. We experience a church service of sorts. My husband breathes deeply, thanking God for the example of strong faith Dad displays in the face of adversity.

> **Cancer does not define you. Your courage in God does.**

Looking down during prayers, I see the silent splashes of tears falling all around our feet. Through watery eyes, I see a freshly formed circle of tears painting a dark watery wreath on the dry cement. My husband chokes up, collecting himself as my mom steps in to talk out loud to God.

What a precious time of prayer and love!

We will cherish "the circle" moment forever.

If you knew my dad before his conversion to faith in Christ, it might surprise you to think of him as a calm and at peace man facing eternity.

It is what it is.

Cancer strikes hard, thrusting into reality. But the power of God brings perfect harmony, washing hearts clean, giving hope for despair.

Do you long for a peace passing all understanding? My dad put his faith in Christ. God may not change your circumstances, but I testify God grants peace in the storm.

You and I can find encouragement by reading all of Philippians. It's packed full of joyful statements, despite Paul writing, chained in a wretched prison.

Despite of terminal cancer, my dad smiles, clasping his cross necklace. We may experience harsh external conditions, but we can cling to internal peace.

God gives the inward courage to rejoice in the Lord always, even gazing downward at a wreath formed of tears . . . on a once-dry cement driveway . . . wrapping arms together . . . in a final group hug.

There's peace in the storm when the Lord nears.

Laura Loveberry

Pass the Baton

"And the things you have heard me say in the presence of many witnesses entrust to reliable men who will also be qualified to teach others."
2 Tim 2:2 NIV

Whatever team triumphs in the medley relay will win the track meet, dancing the trophy overhead, celebrating on the bus ride home. The veins in my forehead stick out. My teeth grind.

Pressure.

As the last leg of this relay race, I twitch, rocking back and forth, biting my lip. Nervously waiting in my lane, the air falls silent.

"On your mark. Get set. BANG!"

Bursting out of the blocks, our first runner bolts toward the curve. The baton handoff times perfectly. Thrusting the baton into the second relay runner's open palm, the teammate speeds around her curve. She pumps her arms rapidly on the backstretch, closing in on her next exchange.

A slight miscommunication ensues.

The awkward handoff slows down our runners. Whipping by, widening a lead, the opposing team passes us. Arms pumping, my third-leg relay member sprints an all-out effort.

The distance between our rival team grows.

The competition rushes by me for a substantial lead, but slows down in their handoff exchange. Their baton pass chops up, losing their momentum.

The shrieks deafen from the crowd, leaning forward, mouths cheering. Teammates for both sides line the infield edge, screaming for their athletes.

I sprint off, feet pounding, arms pumping hard.

"Reach!"

Facing forward, I snap my hand back in full motion, simultaneously grasping the baton thrust into my hand. We swoosh to a near-perfect handoff. Propelling forward at full speed, the surrounding sounds muffle to a surreal softness.

I hear only my breathing.

Racing vigorously, my vision blurs around the edges. My spike shoes pound down the lane. Jousting my facial cheeks, I stride, strenuously battering my arms, driving me onward.

Closing in on my opponent's backside, the screaming teammates flash on the sideline in my peripheral vision. Making my move, I summon all energy, sprinting alongside my opponent.

We dig deep, neck and neck.

Straining forward, the finish line in sight, I thrust both arms down and back. I force my leaning chest across the finish line with nothing left to support my oxygen-depleted legs.

Crossing the line, we both collapse.

Teammates rush, surrounding the finish line. Fist-pumping athletes bounce up and down to a rhythm guided by group dancing and victory chants.

We did it!

We passed the baton without a drop.

We won the race! Triumph results from the training, the gut busting effort, and the teamwork. Those crucial handoffs make the difference, key to the victorious celebration in the end.

It is the same in life.

Don't drop the baton.

Through training, we transfer our faith in Jesus Christ to our children, so they can pass it on to their children and their children's children. Like Paul told Timothy in the Bible, *"What you heard from me, keep as the pattern of sound teaching, with faith and love in Christ Jesus,"* (2 Tim. 1:13 NIV).

> **Do what matters. Pass purpose to the next generation.**

We hold a faith baton to handoff. The race grows strenuous. We can fall behind as parents. But if we focus on this one thing of intentionally training our children, then we prepare them better to pass on our faith to the next generation.

Passing on our faith in Jesus Christ leads to fist-pumping, bouncing up and down, rhythmic group dancing, victory chants by angels in heaven! It's a celebration worthy of a bouncing group-hug swarming with smiles here on earth, too.

Pass the faith on!

Goodbye Chaos Hello Calm

Laura Loveberry

Meek and Wild

". . . for it is God who works in you, to will and to act in order to fulfill his good purpose."
Phil. 2:13 NIV

In my childhood, some demoralizing kids said, "Hey Laura, the Bible says the meek will inherit the kingdom of God. You're not meek. You're not going to heaven."

My eyes pop open.

Since I do not own a Bible, I check this with adults. I ask grownups, "Do you think I am meek?" Nope. They laugh, blurting, "No way!"

Nobody describes me as meek.

This starts my anxiety of not fitting in with meek big-Bible-carrying Christians. In my perception, I am too bold for heaven, so I fear I am going the other direction—hell. Whoa! My ten-year-old face drains to white.

It traumatizes my nights.

Growing to a teenager, I join a Christian club at school that accepts my personality. By faith, I believe in Jesus Christ at a youth gathering. I transform to a full-fledge follower of Jesus understanding he died for my sins to be forgiven and rose so I could live in heaven with him. I walk, bouncing a big smile.

I never fear hell again.

Contemplating my "not-meek-enough" dilemma, I resort to a personality change. This fails. I remain loud and overflowing by nature.

I start reading my Bible daily, attending a Bible-teaching church, and learn to live by God's principles. Eventually, I undergo healthy changes. My personality matures and grows with a God-bent.

I keep my fun-loving ways, but drop my cussing. Quitting my habit of dishonoring God, I no longer say, "Oh my God." Previously, I was using the term repeatedly and disrespectfully.

This verse in Ephesians resonates with me. *"Let no unwholesome word proceed from your mouth, but only such a word as is good for edification according to the need of the moment, so that it will give grace to those who hear,"* (Ephesians 4:29 NASB).

I learn appropriate behavior, developing a sensitivity to God's Holy Spirit guiding me in relationships. My personality remains audacious, not meek by stern-face standards.

I mature, marry, and start a family. God opens a career for me as an inspirational speaker and author with my out-of-the-box personality. With boldness, I share the life-changing power of Jesus Christ to gatherings at Christ-centered events.

Responding enthusiastically, the entertained audiences engage fully because of my high-volume personality and antics. These big-Bible-carrying churches invite me to their events to speak because of my bigger-than-life boldness. The personality I thought did not fit the faith, develops into the trait used to spread the faith.

Plot twist. Ironic, right?

My quandary concerning meekness remains.

I do a word study in the Bible of the term "meek." I learn, in biblical times, meek means "like a wild stallion trained by the master." This is ME.

I AM meek!

I holler to my husband in the other room, who comes running because I sound urgent. Panting with excitement, I explain I am the wild stallion and God trains me. "Master" refers to God. The "wild stallion" denotes me. God, the Master trains me, the wild stallion, and therefore . . . I am MEEK!

> **God created you to SHINE for Jesus.**

He smirks, "You need a bridle sometimes."

Truth.

I howl in laughter, agreeing with a giggle. Often, this mouth of mine gets me into conundrums. I need a mouth guard. A horse's bridle just might work. *Ha.*

I bask in the realization God designed me with this flamboyant personality for God's glory.

God qualifies the unqualified.

My hallelujah, roof-raising response includes dancing and clapping. He trains me, the wild mare, the "meek" one by biblical definition. The Master himself created me and tames me.

"Blessed are the meek, for they shall inherit the earth," (Matthew 5:5 ESV).

My bold personality I once perceived as rejected by Christianity. Now, it's requested for Christian speaking presentations to the glory of God. This unexpected twist I dance to with my moon walk, 80s robot, raising the roof, and a sprawling attempt of the worm dance.

Yes. I went there. I do the worm.

We people with swashbuckling personalities can embrace being meek in a wild-stallion-trained-by-the-Master way. We can glorify God with the bent he created us to live.

Are you a wild stallion running from the training of God? Whoa. Don't buck it. Let the Master train you for his glory. Let God complete you for his glory.

Gallop with God to fulfill your show-stopping destiny!

Goodbye Chaos Hello Calm

Laura Loveberry

Do Right Bugs Bite

". . . not looking to your own interest but each of you to the interest of the others."
Phil. 2:4 NIV

After demanding days of scrubbing, cleaning, and organizing the apartment of a young lady needing guidance, I crawl home exhausted. Cracking a smile of satisfaction, I made a difference.

But I am spent.

Helping others in hard seasons is both fulfilling and draining. I take a deep breath, fill my cheeks with air, and exhale. That was difficult, but it's done.

Or so I thought.

I notice itching around my neck as I go about my morning. I scratch more spots by noontime. By late afternoon, I claw at my neck, arms, belly, buttocks and legs.

Why do I have welts all over?

I cannot take this. Crawling out of my skin, I rush to Emergency Care where I get shots, load up on steroids, and spread a medicinal body crème from head to toe.

As my hives swell, I get a call from the young lady I helped. She called to say she found . . . bedbugs!

I am a highly allergic victim of creepy crawling bites!

What!

I do the research. We hire bedbug searching dogs to inspect our home in case of a parasite transfer. Sure enough, the dogs sniff, going on point at my chair and my bedside.

I shriek!

Evidently, we got bedbugs.

My breathing goes rapid and sweat beads form on my forehead. Immediately, our emergency fund dwindles to pay for a house heat treatment. The prep work to heat treat our huge Victorian home to kill bedbugs and their eggs is massively expensive.

Anxiety crawls around my brain as my fingernails rake the welts covering my body.

My friends cannot risk coming to our home.

Who can blame them? I am not even welcome to sit close to anyone. I am the woman with a scarlet letter "B" for bugs. No one dare hug me. I cannot travel in someone else's car. Flowing tears, I claw my swelled bites, leaving red rows of scratches.

I would never want to risk spreading these nasty bugaboos. They lay up to 250 eggs. I am in full-blown itching anxiety.

I isolate.

One month later, after our house treatment, we hire the bedbug-sniffing dog team again. Trained dogs detect more accurately than humans.

We are bedbug free!

My welts heal! I collapse on my chair in total relief. My face lights up with a smile as my anxiety subsides.

Ministry can be hard.

Costs creep in more than expected. In the thick of serving, you may be hard-pressed with moments of despair. You may sit alone and untouchable.

The price of following God may feel insurmountable.

It may be harder than you can bear on your body, budget, and well-being. When you feel weak, let God be your strength. I admit, I sat shaking my head, overwhelmed by my welts and worry.

But I got back up.

You can, too.

Jesus never quit. Paul pressed on. They released Joseph from prison. You don't have to quit.

> *Even if your body breaks and covers with bruises, don't quit supporting others.*

> *Even if the costs soar high, don't quit giving.*

> *Even if you're exhausted, don't quit trying.*

> *Even if you fall into deep despair, don't quit in the pit.*

> *You and I do not quit.*

Persevere. We can gain empathy and understanding.

Even if the bedbugs bite, don't quit doing RIGHT!

Reflection with a Friend

"The commands of the LORD are radiant,
giving light to the eyes."
Psalm 19:8b KJV

Walking by briskly, someone catches my eye. I snap my head. Dropping my mouth, my eyes open wide. It's my old friend. Whoa!

What messy hair and dark eye circles!

We greet without hugging. It's the new normal since COVID. I see her frizzy hair with an inch of grey roots. Her skin aged since the last time I saw her. Greeting her, I focus on the blemishes and the pull of gravity on her face.

Her saggy wrinkles could use a little lift.

I notice her skin hangs low near the corners of her mouth. I bet it's from smiling. If a person grins broadly and often, their resting face bags southward. I guess it's the price she pays for being a smiler.

She looks different from high school.

Where did her fluttery eyelashes go? She could use mascara, blush, and lipstick. Just saying. And what's up with the roadmap of wrinkling on her neck? She should probably wear a scarf or turtleneck.

I heard some people talking behind her back the other day.

Gazing at her, I know, in part, some gossip fits her. She talks too much, needing to listen more. Often, she's controlling. She's Miss Bossy Pants. And she needs to read her Bible, praying more to stay in tune with God's Spirit.

Dare I confront and pray for her right now? This could be awkward. I'll do it.

She's a hot mess.

I pray out loud for her. Right there, I ask my friend to lay her life before God as an offering. I pray she surrenders her sins, giving her control issues to Jesus. I pray for a new life to emerge, energizing her to walk with Jesus. She needs to transform.

Surprisingly, it's not weird.

The Holy Spirit floats down. We both smile at each other afterwards. I wave goodbye at the exact same time she does. Turning to walk away, I twist back around. She copies me. Invigorated, I smile broadly.

She smiles back.

Her aging wrinkles don't seem as noticeable. Her youthful sparkle returns. Simultaneously, we both grin at each other, and I walk away from my reflection and conversation . . . with the full-view mirror.

Laura Loveberry

Flip Flop Forward

"When he falls, he will not be hurled down,"
Psalm 37:24a NASB

At a fancy pancy country club, I stand in front of an audience of elegant women, listening to my speech. They're reserved. How can I loosen them up a bit? These ladies sit tall, properly dressed in the best attire, flashing diamond rings.

Suddenly, I fidget to adjust to my hidden situation. Evidently, my panty hose released their elasticity, every thread, right in the middle of my message. My eyes widen to the size of quarters.

Ut! Oh!

Maybe stepping to the side will work the sagging hose back upward. Nope. Not a chance. I shuffle like a Walmart shopper testing shoes with a tag attaching the pair. Now, I stumble in two-inch steps, because the crotch on my nylons drops to my knees. It's below my hemline.

My eyes pop open wider.

Sweat drips off my forehead. My mind spins. What's Plan B? Simpering, I announce, "Okay, everyone, turn to someone, telling them you're glad they're here. Tell them Jesus loves them. Give them a hug. I'll be back."

I do my short-step shuffle to the bathroom. Faces crunch, glancing around. Eyes roll down, spotting my baggy ankles. I shake my head back and forth. More sweat rolls. Eyes twitching, I scurry out inch by inch.

Snickers and giggles follow me.

Stumbling into the restroom, I yank off the failed hosiery, looking for a trash can to pitch it. Catching my frazzled face in the mirror, I stop and smirk a grin, nodding my head. I shall jump to Plan B—entertain them with a grand re-entrance.

Strutting full stride back into the ladies' event, holding my hosiery high over my head, I announce, "I'm back, but my hose failed. Ladies, nothing will stop my message!"

I twirl like a ribbon dancer—the hose circling in the air.

The no-longer reserved audience, hoots and hollers. We broke the stuffiness. My applauding audience engages fully during the remaining message. They lean on the edge of their seats. We bond with silliness and laughter.

"Though he fall, he shall not be cast headlong, for the LORD upholds his hand," (Psalm 37:24 ESV).

When we come close to flopping, we can flip it, twirl, and prevail.

Laura Loveberry

As for Me and Mine

". . . then choose for yourselves this day whom you will serve . . ."
Joshua 24:15b NIV

Has your mindset needed a modification over the last couple of years?

Previously, I set two objectives, and both failed. I desired a waterfront house with sunsets and a full speaking schedule to inspire audiences. God's glorious, sun-setting views and encouraging audiences inspire me.

Then the pandemic hit. Boom! Lake house prices soared, and all my speaking events canceled. Bam!

We adjusted.

Unwilling to break our budget, we nixed the lake house after years of searching. We built a garage, and the boring wall became my view. No lake view sunsets. My disappointment weighed me down until I altered my attitude.

As I tell my kids, I flushed my "tude."

Taking action, I painted a pleasant view to lift my spirits and enhance the bare garage wall. I created a mural of our Victorian home adding the Bible verse, *"As for me and my house, we will serve the Lord,"* (Joshua 24:15c NIV). My window view lacks a glorious sunset, but shines for God with my substitute-for-sunset mural. We love it.

Our smiles beam.

My mind shift extended to the little pond my hubster built in our backyard. It's only four feet but hosts goldfish, lily pads, and the occasional frog. I named our petite pond "Lake Laura." Therefore, we own a lakeside dwelling, don't we? *Giggle.* My lake-house mentality took a turn. We created contentment with a petite pond.

We shifted our mindset.

As all major gatherings canceled, I also altered my ministry plan. Instead of speaking, I determined to write inspirational books while earning a ministry degree. My empty event schedule opened my opportunity to accomplish these goals previously put on hold.

Reboot!

My outreach direction shifted. I miss speaking, but pray my books and education will impact others for Christ. Altering my path and adjusting for bumps became an opportunity for me to minister differently. My first novel, *Bowl of Berries Book Club,* inspires sisterhood. With my two nonfiction books, *Invite Delight* and *Goodbye Chaos Hello Calm,* I aspire to encourage readers with positivity.

If we reject sulking over situations, we can create contentment with a mind shift. Bingo!

Are there other areas you and I can use to reposition, rearrange, and recast our vision? Can we amend, adjust, and adapt objectives when calamity hits? Boom. Bam. Reboot. Bingo!

When life takes a spin, we can shift for the win. Our ministry mindset can move the direction of God's U-turns. We can be mindful and amend our map when life flips. Don't flop.

We can dart our desires in new directions.

As for me and my house, we will serve the Lord, adjusting to our happy place with a mural view and a splash of a lake, too.

Laura Loveberry

Halt Hurried Hustle

"Rest in the LORD, and wait patiently for him . . ."
Psalm 37:7a KJV

After listening to a John Mark Comer podcast called "Fight Hustle, End Hurry," I come up with a plan for our home. I thrill to share this, because it could be a game changer in your busy home, too.

Our time is a precious commodity.

We want to be more intentional with our priorities. The premeditated plan will prioritize our home life by scheduling a spouse date night AND a separate spouse "business" night each week.

Monday night is ideal for the short business meeting to discuss issues or troubles, talk about budget spending, and set the agenda for the week. We can dialog about spiritual challenges, too.

My hubster and I used to do weekly date night, and I would address the trouble spots in our marriage. It ended up feeling like the dated dripped with deep work, deflating the fun out.

This new two-different-night focus will keep date night fun, lighthearted, connective, and joyful.

We can discuss the deeper issues, the logistics and weekly schedule at home during the "business" meeting. This keeps date night bonding and playful.

God, family, and ministry need to be a top priority.

Imagine a pile of stones and an empty bucket. Let's say our priorities represent the big rocks we put in an empty bucket. First, we load the important crucial rocks in the bucket (date night, family meal, bible study). Next, we add the extra stones worthy to do, but not a must (girls' night out, euchre night, travel).

When the container fills, it is done. We may find rocks left in our pile not fitting into the bucket. Fine. We intentionally plan our schedule by prioritizing the must-do items.

This plan rocks!

By scheduling our lives intentionally, we make margins to breathe. We keep the main thing the main thing. We plan to live purposefully.

The Bible talks about this. *"Now this is what the LORD Almighty says: "Give careful thought to your ways,"* (Haggai 1:5 NIV).

We can steward our time wisely.

We keep the best "yes" and let the "no" go. Not all pebbles from the pile go in the bucket. Giving thought to our ways is a worthy phrase. You and I desire to live a contemplative life with less rushing.

Ironically, I am currently in panic-mode proofreading this, busily bouncing and burping my grandchild. I sweat about all the things I need to accomplish before I fly out the door for a three-day speaking tour starting today. And I just now excitedly answered "yes" to a phone call to speak at a ladies' event.

Ha. Ha. Ha.

My hustle hurried home needs to take this to heart!

Laura Loveberry

Bitter or Better

"Fathers, do not provoke your children to anger by the way you treat them. Rather, bring them up with the discipline and instruction that comes from the Lord."
Ephesians 6:4 NLT

Channel surfing, I come across a desperate woman sobbing in a courtroom spouting something like this, "Please, I beg you. It's all my fault. I poisoned my baby's mind during our horrid divorce. I planted hate, exaggerating story after sad story. My boy only heard the bad side about my ex-husband. I lied because I hurt. It's my fault and my emotional mess. Please convict me of murder instead. I drove my son to murder. I poisoned his mind against his father."

I cannot pull away.

Sitting dead silent, the courtroom listens to this wailing mother plead for herself to go to jail for the rest of her life instead of her son. He obviously pulled the trigger. The guilty boy's distraught momma blows snot, floods tears, and pleads to take her son's place.

Every parent should watch this courtroom recording.

It is a wake-up call for parents to be aware of the influence they have on their child. Do not risk planting a seed of bitterness in your child who could grow up deplorably bitter, mean, and even seek unjust revenge.

What a tragic waste of a teachable time for the parent. The damage shows clearly as the boy's life will be behind bars.

The mom lives in a prison of her own guilt.

It need not be this way.

Let's compare this scene with a letter I read. A young lady wrote a beautiful tribute to her relative who passed away. She shared how this relative loved her much, and she cherishes the special memories.

The tribute shone with positivity. The writer meant every single word, depicting her love for this family member. Not an ounce of hate exists, not a sliver.

But I know her parents and her situation.

The deceased relative left this young lady out of many family events. He owned a recreational vehicle, taking her cousins out on it, but not her. He bought tickets to events, taking all the family kids, but not her.

His gift giving to family was disproportionate.

Some might call it favoritism against her.

The parents of the little girl did not understand the disparity with their child and this family member, but they did not feed it and poison the relationship. They downplayed it when their daughter asked when it would be her turn to go.

The parents simply reminded their little girl, this relative loved her, and the parents did not plant hate ever. They chose better and were not bitter, so she did not have emotional scars.

Their daughter overflows with love for the deceased relative to this day.

Compare these two scenes.

One parent fed hatred to their child, who swallowed it deep into destruction. Another child's parents nourished with love, and the child loves unconditionally with a pure heart.

Parents can use teachable moments to instill love, instead of hate, to grow character and forgiveness, instead of bitterness and revenge.

It's a choice.

". . . I have set before you life and death, blessings and curses. Now choose life, so that you and your children may live and that you may love the LORD your God, listen to his voice, and hold fast to him . . ." (Deuteronomy 30: 19b-20a NIV).

Parents influence children.

Choose your impact wisely.

Laura Loveberry

Goodbye Chaos. Hello Calm.

*"For the world offer . . . a craving for everything we see,
and pride in our achievements and possessions. These are
not from the Father, but are from this world."*
1 John 2:19 NLT

Do you live in chaos? Do you sigh, rolling your eyes at your messy house?

Not too long ago, we lived in a chaotic home. I breathed uneasily, my heart thudded, and frowning overtook my face at the disorder of my space. Facing major stress in my family, I determined to focus on simplifying my life. I cannot control the family circumstance, but I can ease the stress levels in my physical environment.

I committed to simplify our living space.

An organized friend spent a day inside my closet. We sorted out clothes that no longer fit, are not my color, and not flattering on me. I pitched clothes I do not love. The worn, itchy, or uncomfortable get tossed. Clothes go into one of four boxes: giveaway-to-friend box, throwaway box, give-to-charity box, sell box.

She teaches me to face all shirts in the same direction. I line up clothing from light to dark colors and then from sleeveless to short-sleeve to long sleeve. Hanging like items together adds order. I purchase all black velvet hangers with no-slip, narrow space-saving uniformity.

The organization delights!

Less is more.

Walking into my closet ignites absolute joy now. My insides twirl like a spinning girl in a new flowing skirt. I converted a small bedroom into my make-up station, jewelry, and clothing-center hub. Painstakingly, I sorted out every piece of makeup and jewelry I did not love, did not wear, or deemed out of style.

I tossed out a mini-mountain.

Next, starting with the easiest, I continue to sort one room at a time completely. Removing everything from the space, I put back properly only what I deeply cherish and use.

Keeping boxes on hand marked *TOSS, KEEP, REGIFT, ATTIC, FIX LATER, CHARITY* simplifies the process. Don't start without them. If using plastic bags, choose the color black, so you and your family won't peek, tempting to keep the useless clutter.

In the kitchen, the land-of-misfits, I sorted with vengeance. Emptying every drawer, I scattered everything on the floor and counters. The sea of unnecessary, not-often-used kitchen items fills boxes for charity. I kept only items I used that matched and that fit in the drawer.

All oddball, plastic containers of various shapes and sizes, I dumped and replaced with a lid-matching storage system. Traveling cups, I narrowed down to ten with matching lids, throwing out the remaining thirty-three. Twenty-seven crusty, stained hot pads I tossed, keeping the two silicone, easy-to-clean oven mitts. Seventeen failed, melted spatulas jammed in one wobbly drawer. I replaced them with two excellent-working silicone spatulas.

I kept the top-ten pots and pans, and the losers went bye-bye. Random glasses filled the charity-to-go box. I kept only the matching sets.

I tossed out dated food.

Do I trust the spice with an expiration date of 1984? No. That spice-filled-jar gift from our wedding, thirty-five years beyond the end date, I chuck it. Check the termination dates and pitch, pitch, pitch.

I cleared out the food item if the box's contents need chiseling to access. You do not want to know about the itsy-bitsy creatures crawling inside the flour bag lost in the recesses of the cupboard. Shriek!

Terrified, I tossed it out.

Whew!

Organization wins with a designated place for everything in all kitchen cupboards. The drawers roll shut with ease, bringing a smile to my sweating face as I plop on the floor, blowing out a laborious sigh.

This takes time and back-aching effort.

Sort your attic last.

Trust me. It overwhelms. Take photos of memorable items and perhaps pass on to others. If you didn't use an item for ten years, do you keep it? You don't need it.

Be free from storing it.

Over the years, I decluttered our entire home on three separate occasions, starting from the easiest room and move to the hardest. With each purging, the layers of clutter became even more minimal.

Reading books about declutter helps with motivation.

Freedom from visual stress creates a home retreat for the mind to rest, enjoying, and soaking in the bliss. I stretch my legs, leaning my recliner back with my hands behind my head, smiling in tranquility. I sigh with relief.

Ahh! I live in a relaxing environment.

With less mess-distraction, I focus on God's calling—to encourage others through writing and speaking. Big Bonus! I make room for a delightful, prayer-chair space for my morning devotions. I even created a presentation on

Decluttering Your Home and Heart to speak at women's events.

The Bible refers to a season to save and a period to pitch out. *"There is a time for everything . . . A time to keep and a time to throw away."* (Ecclesiastics 3:1a, 6b NASB).

We handle outside pressures better when our home is in order. You and I can do it.

Goodbye chaos. Hello calm. *

This chapter repeats from my first book in my set. I include this topic again because it inspired the title suiting this second book. Decluttering my entire home three different times, I reread these insights worth repeating to help the process of minimizing.

Laura Loveberry

Worst Day Best Day

"Blessed are those who mourn, for they shall be comforted."
Matt. 5:4 NIV

Have you been at a loss for words when talking to a friend who is missing a loved one who passed?

Often, I pray for the Lord to give me the words to speak so I can comfort grievers. The other day, I heard a remarkable statement on the radio by a widowed woman, causing me to ponder each word. I want to remember her words to share at just the right time.

The opportunity comes soon.

The next day, I meet an acquaintance whose husband died. I remember this couple as a strong Christian pair, loving Jesus.

> **I find comfort my worst day is your BEST DAY EVER.**

Giving her a hug as we talk, I share the comment I heard on the radio earlier.

As believers, I remind her, "Your worst day ever is your husband's best day ever." Looking pensive, she asks me to repeat what I just said.

"Your worst day ever is your husband's best day ever," I say again.

Smiling softly, she states, "I will always remember this. I processed the words for a moment, but it rings true. It's comforting."

We both acknowledge her husband left the earth, but because of his faith in Jesus Christ, he goes directly to be with God. He experienced the exceedingly best day ever—no more suffering, struggle, or pain. He ran to Jesus, embraced in the biggest bear hug.

Pensively, she mentions another "worst day ever" in her life when a grandchild drowned. The truth comforts her heart for that loss, too.

Death's sting is not the end for those holding faith in Christ. It's the new beginning. For a committed follower of Jesus Christ, death opens the doorway into the best day ever.

Those who remain on earth miss them desperately, but our faithful departed love ones celebrate with Jesus in glorified bodies. It's their "mostest, bestest" day ever.

You heard of the book title, *Alexander and the Terrible, Horrible, No Good, Very Bad Day*. Well, we can experience terribly rotten, worthless, horrifically painful, overwhelming, hard, bad, uber bad, stinky overbearingly, and heartbreaking days.

In the book of John, we read, *"For God so loved the world that he gave his only son, that whoever believes in him will not perish but have eternal life,"* (John 3:16 NIV). To not perish but experience eternal life means living forever with Jesus. It's true.

Jesus remains the way, the truth, and the life.

My friend will now remember her worst day on earth as her loved ones' heavenly best day ever.

This truth may encourage others in need of a ray of light in a dark time.

Laura Loveberry

Missing Peace of a Masterpiece

"For we are God's masterpiece . . ."
Eph. 2:10a NLT

Is something missing in your life?

Do you long for a relationship to give you peace, purpose, and passionate belonging? Do you know God loves you with your personality, faults, and failures?

It matters not how long we ran away from right. It only matters we put our faith in the one True God through Jesus Christ.

Believing in the God of the Bible doesn't promise us a laid-back life. My life got harder when I put my faith in Jesus, but God gives me the muscle to climb upward. I study the Bible, talking to God (praying), building friendships with believers, and growing in Bible-teaching churches.

> **You cannot be fully you without Jesus. He is your missing peace.**

In Jesus, I find peace, purpose, and a passionate belonging with an out-of-the box, over-the-top and I-will-overcome zest for life in Christ!

Is your life missing a piece?

I spelled "piece" correctly. Is something absent from your life? You cannot be fully you without Jesus. Christ completes us.

The Bible states Jesus is the Way, the Truth, and the Life.

You can talk to God, believing in Jesus Christ based on this Bible verse. *"For God so loved the world that he gave his one and only Son, that whoever believes in him shall not perish but have eternal life,"* (John 3:16 NIV).

In the book of Ephesians, the Bible explains we cannot work our way to heaven being good enough because faith is a free gift, not earned. *"For it is by grace you have been saved, through faith — and this is not from yourselves, it is the gift of God — not by works, so that no one can boast,"* (Eph. 2:8-9 NIV).

Today, you can talk to God, putting your faith in Jesus. Our goodness matters not. Jesus forgives our sins because he loves us enough to die to pay the price of our forgiveness. We trust this by faith.

Jesus loves YOU. *JESUS loves you.* JESUS LOVES YOU!

I got saved.

Saved from what? Saved from my sins and saved from death. Jesus paid the penalty for my sin and the hell I deserved. I was prideful, controlling, and used the Lord's name badly. Now, I hold the promise of eternal life. I'm forgiven. This means heaven with Jesus when I die.

How did I become a Christian? How do you become a Christian?

Simply believe. Believe in Jesus Christ.

Trust in Jesus. Faith in Jesus makes you a follower of Christ. It's not magical words repeated. Nope. It's not working hard enough. It's not.

Understand you and I are sinners in need of a Savior. It's simply believing in Jesus.

Jesus came. Jesus died. Jesus rose. Jesus lives.

That's God's explanation of the plan for you.

To be redeemed means that Jesus died in exchange for the payment of your sins. I turned from my sin and wrapped around God's forgiveness. Some call this repenting of sin. When you embrace this concept of Christ paying for your sin, Jesus releases you from guilt.

What freedom!

Do you believe in Jesus?

Right now, you can decide to believe in Jesus by faith. I suggest rereading this chapter and praying it through with God. Believe! Faith in Jesus Christ makes you a genuine follower. Before you close this book, you can become a Christian with a new life.

Perhaps you will ponder this Bible-based prayer I prayed when I first trusted in Jesus Christ. It went something like the prayer below. If God speaks to your heart, I encourage you to get genuine with God right now.

"Dear God, I am a sinner. The penalty for my sin is death. Thank you for sending Jesus to die on the cross for me, so Jesus can forgive my sins. He paid in full. Thank you for Jesus rising from the dead, so I can embrace eternal life and live forever in heaven with YOU. Right now, I put my faith in Jesus Christ. I believe in Jesus. Thank you for saving me. In Jesus' name, I pray, Amen."

I added, "Please don't make me a Jesus Freak," but God transformed me into one. The "Jesus Freak" label I wear proudly to this day!

I finally stopped running from him. By faith, I believe in Jesus. I embraced God's plan. I trusted in Jesus and got saved. You can, too.

Take a "selah" moment. Pause. Reflect. You can communicate with God and believe in Jesus right now. You may choose to pray the prayer I wrote a few paragraphs earlier, or use your own words.

(Selah Prayer Pause)

I pray you became a believer today.

If you became a Christian today, congratulations! All heaven celebrates! You're encouraged you to study your Bible daily, talk to God often, and worship in a Bible-teaching church. I do. I love it!

Before I converted to a follower of Christ, I experienced a void, a missing piece in my life. I missed peace.

Now, God fills the empty place and peace overflows.

In the book of Ephesians, I came across the Bible verse, *"For we are God's masterpiece. He has created us anew in Christ Jesus, so we can do the good things he planned for us long ago,"* (Eph. 2:10 NLT).

I discovered God's design plan preparing us in advance to live out our God-driven calling. He forms us uniquely for his service.

When you believe in God, you discover God creates you as his workmanship. He planned you in advance. He designed you as his creation.

God's an artist.

You are his masterpiece.

As a true believer, you can paint your world with the personality God created. You can say goodbye to any confusion in your mind and say hello to God's calm serenity. You can share your faith in the style God fashioned you!

You be YOU. . .

>fully at peace . . .

>>not missing a piece . . .

>>>God's complete masterpiece!

Laura Loveberry

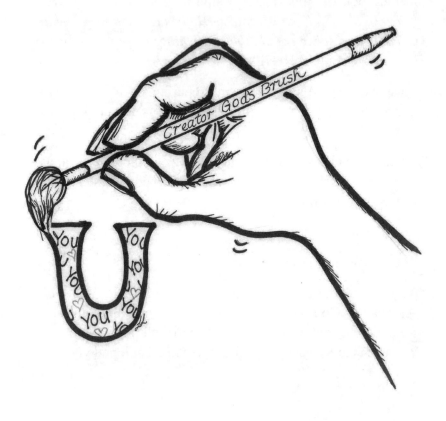

Goodbye Chaos

"Cast all your anxiety on him because he cares for you"
1 Peter 5:7 NIV

With God, we can open the door, smiling as we usher in the calm. We wave goodbye to the chaos. It doesn't need to come inside. Becoming a Christian unlocks the key to centered living in a chaotic world.

God calms our anxious hearts when we read his Word.

You and I can write down verses, finding our refuge. We can read them out loud. We can repeat them until we memorize the rescuing words.

I close *Goodbye Chaos Hello Calm* with a powerful selah moment brought to you by the psalmist David. He penned these verses to inspire Christians to say goodbye to the outward confusion and welcome the inward peace.

With God, we can know peace no matter the troubles.

No God. No peace.

Know God. Know peace.

"God is our refuge and strength, and ever-present help in trouble. Therefore, we will not fear, though the earth give way and the mountains fall into the heart of the sea, though its waters roar and foam and the mountains quake with their surging . . . He says, 'Be still, and know that I am God; I will be exalted among the nations, I will be exalted in the earth.' The Lord Almighty is with us; the God of Jacob is our fortress," (Psalm 46:1-3 and 10-11 NIV).

Christians can take their confusion, calamites, and catastrophes to God. He calms our conundrums. Reading his Word rewards us with a refuge. He gives us purpose, passion, and peace in the pandemonium.

"So do not fear for I am with you; do not be dismayed, for I am your God. I will strengthen you and help you . . ." (Isaiah 41:10a NIV).

God doesn't always change our chaotic circumstances, but he can grant us calm, kicking the chaos out of our minds. We have access to his fortitude, resilience, valor, steadfastness, tenacity, perseverance, resolve, and determination. It's ours for the taking.

Grab God's grit. Do it.

It's a battle of the mind.

We can find 365+ phrases stating the concept "do not fear" in the Bible. That's one shot of bravery for every day of the year. This helps us quell our nervous hearts.

Waving goodbye to the mayhem involves understanding God is large and in charge. *"When I am afraid, I put my trust in you."* (Psalm 56:3 NIV). Trust him.

He is trustworthy.

I thank the Lord for reaching down to me, relieving my anxiety. Check out this encouragement. *"I waited patiently for the Lord; he inclined unto me and heard my cry, He brought me up also out of a horrible pit, out of the miry clay, and set my feet upon a rock, and established my goings. And he hath put a new song in my mouth, even praise unto our God . . ."* (Psalm 40:1-3a KJV).

While experiencing dangerous trauma, that verse is now my testimony of victorious overcoming. I crawled my way out of my pit.

Literally, I walked with Jesus around a high school track, quoting verse after uplifting Bible verse, renewing my mind. Pounding around the track, sometimes all I could speak out loud to God was, "God. Oh God. Oh GOD!"

Tearing up as I type, I remember how he set me free of paralyzing anxiety. Through circling the oval with him outside in his creation, I renewed my mind with his scriptures. Thankfully, I memorized key verses before my traumatic season of turmoil. It's crucial to read the Word.

We cannot recall verses we never read.

My mind renewed by repeating God's truths.

Jesus walked beside me around the track.

Clinging in desperation, my relationship with God tightened.

I do not miss that season living in danger, but I appreciate the closeness of living fully dependent on God for every step I attempted to take. Those desperate days led to deeper dependence, real reliance, and powerful praise.

A part of me misses the closeness to God in my unbearable season, but I never want to live through the gut-wrenching trauma again. God's presence astounds me.

He marched me through the battlefield in my mind.

Jesus walked and talked often with his disciples, too.

It's healthy. You and I can walk with Jesus, singing praise to our God, lifting our serotonin levels naturally. We can memorize and repeat God's worthy words of insight. Physically walking with Jesus exercises our bodies. As modern-day disciples, it can be our restoration route.

The verses in this chapter provide inspiration worth planting in our hearts as we stride along. These scriptures offer strength for climbing out of a pit. Equipping our hearts for battle, it is wise to memorize verses of fortitude.

Casting my cares on God gives me contentment. I don't need to be living constantly in chaos. *"So be content with who you are, and don't put on airs. God's strong hand is on you; he'll promote you at the right time. Live carefree before God; he is most careful with you,"* (1 Peter 5-7 MSG).

Saying good riddance to calamity takes discernment and wisdom. The Bible is clear, *"If any of you lacks wisdom, you should ask God, who gives generously to all without finding fault, and it will be given to you,"* (James 1:5 NIV).

Remember, Jesus did not burden himself with a home overflowing with possessions. Limiting our consumerism, enjoying the "more of less," we can downsize, declutter, and "dejunk" our overabundant stuff. Freeing us to focus on following Jesus, we can serve with fewer distractions.

"Then he said to them, 'Watch out! Be on your guard against all kinds of greed; life does not consist in an abundance of possessions," (Luke 12:15 NIV).

Get rid of the excess. Make your house a refuge.

You and I can then relax, rest, and renew in our home.

We can focus on what matters. Love God. Love People. By saying hello to Jesus and goodbye to things, we can do what we heard. You and I can live the Word with less worry and more prayer.

Above my widowed mom's bed, I painted, "Worry Less. Pray More." It reminds her to trust God, pray for her requests, and worry less. This concept comes from the following verse.

"Don't worry about anything; instead, pray about everything. Tell God what you need, and thank him for all he has done. Then you will experience God's peace, which exceeds anything we can understand. His peace will guard your hearts and minds as you live in Christ Jesus," (Phil 4:6-7 NLT).

"Therefore do not worry about tomorrow, for tomorrow will worry about itself. Each day has enough trouble of its own," (Matt 6:34 NIV).

Saying goodbye to the world's worries is as simple as this verse explains, *"I am leaving you with a gift—peace of mind and heart. And the peace I give is a gift the world cannot give. So don't be troubled or afraid,"* (John 14:17 NLT).

Read. Rest. Recoup. Restore. Revive.

"I'm not saying that I have this all together, that I have it made. But I am well on my way, reaching out for Christ, who has so wondrously reached out for me. Friends, don't get me wrong: By no means do I count myself an expert in all of this, but I've got my eye on the goal, where God is beckoning us onward – to Jesus . . ." (Phil. 13:12-14a MSG).

Some negative circumstances might not change, but our positive mindset can improve, focusing on Christ. I can try to fix the surrounding situation and fail, but God can bless in the mess.

Sometimes we need a God-centered mindset shift.

We can pray it through for our breakthrough.

Saying goodbye to the confusion and hello to tranquility is like joining Jesus for a lovely stroll along a clear path through an overgrown mess of a garden. It's sitting peacefully beside Jesus on a park bench while the world hustles and bustles around us. It's like tuning into deep conversations with the Lord while the noisy clatter of the park fades away with each insight Jesus reveals.

Letting go of distractions and bonding with Jesus satisfies our spiritual longing, restoring our souls.

It's like sitting with Jesus . . .

renewing our inmost self . . .

calming our lives to serve well . . .

no matter the chaotic setting.

Breathe in Jesus. Exhale jitters. Gulp the glorious life.

Find a moment to fully surrender your ways to his will, face down on the floor, just you and the Lord. I do this. God swoops down and lifts me up.

Today, I pray for you and me to live fruitful lives, loving God and loving people, saying, "Goodbye outward chaos. Hello inward calm."

Laura Loveberry

99 Life Coach Questions
Goodbye Chaos. Hello Calm.

1. Describe a time when your life got splattered.
2. How do you stay calm in chaotic moments?
3. What unexpected situations caught you off guard?
4. Describe a memorable first date ending in calamity.
5. What kind of chef or cook are you?
6. What are your strengths and weakness?
7. How do you treat your Bible? Do you underline or write in the margins? Do you keep it unmarked?
8. Describe a time when you experienced estrangement from someone you love.
9. Describe your reaction to Jesus if he came in today to talk to you.
10. What change would happen if you walked with Jesus all day?
11. How often do you share your faith?
12. When you sin, how do you handle it?
13. Would your sin abhor God?
14. How do you look at other people's sin?
15. Describe a time you waited long for prayers to be answered.
16. What prayer are you still waiting to be answered?
17. Describe your best birthday gift ever.
18. Jesus chose 12 men to mentor. Who would you like to mentor, and why?
19. Do you feel qualified to share your faith?
20. How would you approach sharing your testimony?

21. Describe a time you ever sunk into a pit.
22. Describe a humorous moment when everything went amuck.
23. Who's your favorite Bible overcoming verse? Why?
24. Describe some knots in your tapestry of life.
25. Describe an event you regretted, but God used as a later blessing.
26. How does God see you?
27. Describe a pivot point in your life.
28. Describe a consequence you avoided with a wise decision, but a hard choice.
29. How can we pray for this next generation?
30. What is your biggest "up" in life?
31. What is your biggest "down" in life?
32. How does God carry you through the ups and downs?
33. Describe a time you were in public and something was amiss with your outfit or face.
34. Does your family greet and depart with kisses?
35. Does your spouse or friends notice when you have something in your teeth?
36. Do you tell others if something is amiss or let it go?
37. Describe a time you needed the Lord to pull you up.
38. What happened in your past that makes you appreciate your present?
39. What are you grateful for?
40. What is your best advice for marriage or dating?
41. What encourages your heart in relationships?
42. Are you a romantic soul? How about your spouse or friends?
43. Do you stop and pray for strangers?

44. Where is the strangest place you ever prayed for another person?
45. Can you name a time you felt compelled to pray for a stranger?
46. What is your opinion about networking?
47. What is your opinion about multi-level marketers?
48. How do you approach sharing your faith?
49. Does your past affect your future?
50. How do past life-styles affect your present?
51. Describe what forgiveness means to you.
52. What's your favorite romantic movie and why?
53. What's romantic?
54. How do you make your spouse or friends feel special?
55. Describe your worst day ever?
56. How do you pull out of a bad day?
57. What is your favorite psalm in the Book of Psalms?
58. What do you do to create calm?
59. What is your favorite stay-calm-and-carry-on quote?
60. Who is the calmest in your relationships?
61. When has God given you strength beyond yourself?
62. What is one of your hardest things to overcome?
63. Name a time when others let you down?
64. Name a prayer God answered with a "no."
65. What is your hardest unanswered prayer?
66. Are you in God's will right now?
67. Name something God kept from you for your good.
68. Name something God gave you unexpectedly for your good.
69. Describe a time God called you to do something you did not want to try.

70. How do you help people with terminal illness?
71. Have you ever been with someone when they passed?
72. How do you minister to others in troubled times?
73. Who are people of faith in your family?
74. Do you have the same faith as your parents?
75. How do you intentionally pass your faith to your children, grandchildren, or relatives?
76. What is your personality type?
77. Would you like to change your personality?
78. How can God use your personality for his glory?
79. What was your hardest experience in ministry?
80. Have you ever experienced bedbugs? Are you careful at hotels to check for bugs?
81. How can you minister to people of lower means?
82. What do you see when you look in the mirror?
83. How do wrinkles affect your mindset?
84. How do you encourage yourself when you are exhausted?
85. Do you meet regularly to discuss business side of marriage? Would it benefit you?
86. Do you have a date night? What do you enjoy?
87. What are your common interests as a couple or with friends?
88. What do you do with bitterness?
89. Do you know people with a bitter heart? How can you impact them?
90. What is the hardest thing you had to forgive?
91. Does your home need to be decluttered or is it organized?
92. Would you benefit from decluttering your home and, if so, how would you approach it?

Goodbye Chaos Hello Calm

93. What does minimalist mean to you?
94. Describe your deepest loss through death.
95. How do you handle the death of a loved one?
96. How do you move forward in grief?
97. Do you have a missing piece or a void in your life? If so, describe it. If not, what fills your void?
98. How does one become a Christian?
99. Are you a Christian? Why or why not?

Laura Loveberry

Laura Loveberry

BOWL OF BERRIES BOOK CLUB

A Sweet Sistahood Novel

LAURA LOVEBERRY

Goodbye Chaos Hello Calm

INVITE DELIGHT

Insights to Sweeten the Soul

LAURA LOVEBERRY

Laura Loveberry

Laura's Library

School Based:

Splatter Paint Hero Special Edition — Kids laugh while reading Arty's antics and learning the color wheel. This full-color hardcover includes bonus cartooning lessons.

Splatter Paint Hero Activity Book — Young readers love coloring the story, drawing step by step, and enjoying art activities in this compact paperback version.

Paint Splat Hero — It's a silly story teaching color theory. Kids love this full-color paperback.

Cartoon It — This delightful paperback shares Arty's overcoming story of learning to draw funny faces. A bonus caricature drawing course is included.

Faith Based:

Caricature It — Faith-based caricature course for ALL AGES.

Laura's Women's Library

A Sweet Sisterhood Novel

In **Bowl of Berries Book Club**, who could imagine a variety of women trapped in a vault with a tattooed dude? No one. But a book club sprouts out of a botched bank robbery, a bowl of berries, and a brand-new book. Their bond grows. As their lives intertwine, will their deep-rooted secrets, shocking twists, and crazy adventures prune them? Will they cultivate fruitful lives after digging deep into their past? What would you find unlocking the vault of your soul?
Five complete strangers are about to find out.

Insights to Soothe the Soul

Goodbye Chaos Hello Calm is a welcoming read of standalone chapters with refreshing encouragement. Open the door to hope and humor. Hug hello to happiness even in the hard. Discover peace under pressure. This delightful giftbook packs with insights for fruitful living.

Insights to Sweeten the Soul

Invite Delight offers hope, humor, and heartfelt encouragement. Find tips to transform. Savor insights to craft the life you crave. Laugh with Laura. Sista, say hello to happy in the hard. These aha standalone chapters challenge us to better ourselves. It's a perfect pick-me-up gift for friends.

Laura Loveberry

Want a Lively Speaker for your next event?

Laura Loveberry
is
available to speak
at
Church Events, Conferences, Outreaches, & Women Retreats.

www.LauraLoveberry.com

Laura Loveberry

Laura Loveberry
SPEAKER   AUTHOR   LIFE COACH

Dr. Laura Loveberry captivates women at conferences and retreats nationwide. Laura's speaking ignites with high energy and drama. She delights audiences, adding sign-language set to music. Laura creates workout DVDs and writes inspirational books with wit and wisdom for women. Her *Life is the Berries* magazine articles reach 1000s monthly. To connect with Laura for your speaking event visit: *www.LauraLoveberry.com*

Laugh with Laura school visits promote literacy and learning as she shares her children's art books. Laura delights in drawing 100s of caricatures at schools, corporate events, festivals, and receptions. For booking contact: *www.SplatterPaintHero.com*

As a former *Mrs. Michigan America*, Laura now crowns herself "Glamma" to her three grandkids. With family a golf cart ride away, Laura and hubster Mark Loveberry live "BERRY" blessed in a quaint village in Michigan.

loveberrylk@gmail.com
www.lauraloveberry.com
www.splatterpainthero.com

Laura Loveberry

Available Women's Books:

Bowl of Berries Book Club
A Sweet Sisterhood Novel

Invite Delight
Insights to Sweeten the Soul

Goodbye Chaos Hello Calm
Insights to Soothe the Soul

Fit for a Queen
Health & Weight-loss Book

Available Children's Art Education Picture Books:

Splatter Paint Hero Special Edition
Kids Laugh & Learn the Color Wheel

Splatter Paint Hero Activity Book
Kids Color the Story & Draw Step by Step

Paint Splat Hero
Kids Laugh & Learn Color Theory

Cartoon It
Silly Story and Step-by-Step Caricatures

Available Faith-based Art Book:

Caricature It
Step-by-Step Caricature Course for All Ages

Available Workout DVDS & Music CD:

Walk the Talk Workout DVD
Easy Breezy Walking with Weights

Wholehearted Living Workout DVD
Advanced Aerobics with Weights

Silent Witness Break Free CD

Laura Loveberry

GOODBYE CHAOS HELLO CALM
Insights to Soothe the Soul

Could this book open a new outlook?

Hug hello to happy! Open the door to hope and humor even in the hard. It's a welcoming read of standalone chapters to encourage and equip. Find peace under pressure. This refreshing gift book packs with insights for fruitful living. See ya later sour. Hi ya sweet. Laugh a little. Love the uplift. Lean into the LIGHT. Book clubs appreciate the life-coaching questions.

> Enjoy the read like a bowl of berries . . .
> double-dipped in chocolate . . .
> delivered on a hectic day! Ahh!

"I love it! Readers will connect with Laura's tenacious faith, earthiness, and humor. Her great content will grab readers."
Ann Spangler, Award-winning Writer & Best-selling Author

Dr. Laura Loveberry

Dr. Laura Loveberry, national conference and retreat speaker, writes witty books inspiring women to overcome. Laura draws 100s of caricatures at school and community events, offering art books for kids. *www.lauraloveberry.com.*